Cambridge Elements

Elements in Music, 1600–1750
edited by
Rebecca Herissone
University of Manchester
Daniel R. Melamed
Indiana University (Emeritus)

LETTERA AMOROSA

Musical Love Letters in Early Modern Italy

Roseen Giles
Duke University

Shaftesbury Road, Cambridge CB2 8EA, United Kingdom

One Liberty Plaza, 20th Floor, New York, NY 10006, USA

477 Williamstown Road, Port Melbourne, VIC 3207, Australia

314–321, 3rd Floor, Plot 3, Splendor Forum, Jasola District Centre, New Delhi – 110025, India

103 Penang Road, #05–06/07, Visioncrest Commercial, Singapore 238467

Cambridge University Press is part of Cambridge University Press & Assessment, a department of the University of Cambridge.

We share the University's mission to contribute to society through the pursuit of education, learning and research at the highest international levels of excellence.

www.cambridge.org
Information on this title: www.cambridge.org/9781009517447

DOI: 10.1017/9781009446808

© Roseen Giles 2025

This publication is in copyright. Subject to statutory exception and to the provisions of relevant collective licensing agreements, no reproduction of any part may take place without the written permission of Cambridge University Press & Assessment.

When citing this work, please include a reference to the DOI 10.1017/9781009446808

First published 2025

A catalogue record for this publication is available from the British Library

ISBN 978-1-009-51744-7 Hardback
ISBN 978-1-009-44678-5 Paperback
ISSN 2755-9726 (online)
ISSN 2755-9718 (print)

Additional resources for this publication at www.cambridge.org/lettera-amorosa

Cambridge University Press & Assessment has no responsibility for the persistence or accuracy of URLs for external or third-party internet websites referred to in this publication and does not guarantee that any content on such websites is, or will remain, accurate or appropriate.

Lettera amorosa

Musical Love Letters in Early Modern Italy

Elements in Music, 1600–1750

DOI: 10.1017/9781009446808
First published online: February 2025

Roseen Giles
Duke University
Author for correspondence: Roseen Giles, roseen.giles@duke.edu

Abstract: In early modern Italy, letters were not only written and read but, in some cases, sung. Musical settings of love letters rekindled a complex kind of vocality which was rooted in the letters of antiquity and endured in the musical subgenre of the *lettera amorosa*. Epistolary poetry served to transform, or, to echo Achillini's *lettera* set by Monteverdi (1567–1643), to 'distill' a lover's thoughts and emotions into verse, and the music that set it was equally transformative. The history of musical letters spans several centuries. It begins in the early sixteenth century with a setting of Ovid's *Heroides* by Tromboncino; returns in the early seventeenth century through the *lettere amorose* of Monteverdi, D'India, and Frescobaldi; and ends with epistolary cantatas by Carissimi, Melani, and Domenico Scarlatti. This Element traces the breadth and significance of the musical love letter with a focus on the provocative *lettere amorose* of the seventeenth century.

Keywords: Claudio Monteverdi, lettera amorosa, love letters, seventeenth-century music, madrigals

© Roseen Giles 2025

ISBNs: 9781009517447 (HB), 9781009446785 (PB), 9781009446808 (OC)
ISSNs: 2755-9726 (online), 2755-9718 (print)

Contents

Preface	1
Prologue	1
1 Voices of Antiquity	9
2 The Epistolary Madrigal	23
3 Monteverdi's Love Letters	41
4 *Lettera amorosa* in the Seventeenth Century	59
5 The Epistolary Cantata	78
Epilogue	89
Bibliography	91

Preface

The poetic transcriptions, translations, and music examples presented here are meant primarily for study and not as critical editions of the texts. Some basic editorial principles have been followed. In the Italian texts, most spellings have been modernized, as has the historical practice of capitalization of some nouns save in circumstances in which the meaning is ambiguous or obscured. Similarly, accents have also been omitted to follow modern practice except where they are necessary to clarify the presence of certain verb forms.

Many of the music examples, the pieces for solo voice in recitative style especially, do not have consistent bar lines in their original prints. The transcriptions given here follow bar lines present in the partbooks, if any, and otherwise provide them at the breve or semibreve to clarify the musical and poetic lines. Repeated accidentals are given just as they appear in the partbooks and where they are not, the convention of holding an accidental through the end of a bar applies. No *basso continuo* figures, other than those appearing in the original prints, have been added.

Prologue

Johannes Vermeer's 'The Love Letter' is remarkably small, a mere 44 cm by 38.5 cm, yet remarkably curious. The painting depicts a richly dressed woman and her maidservant in what appears to be a domestic space (Figure 1). The perspective is unusual. The viewer is not in the same room as the subjects, as the foreground of the painting is an open doorway with a drawn curtain revealing the brighter scene in the next room. To the right of the darkened doorway is a chair upon which rests crumpled sheets of music; to the left is a large map along the wall. The seated woman is holding a cittern in one hand, as if she were playing but a moment ago, and an unopened letter in the other. She looks up at her maidservant with an expression which could convey both relief and anticipation. The painted seascapes above her head suggest that the letter comes from afar and from someone very important to her. While the situation implies that the maidservant has just delivered the letter to her lady, the musical imagery in this painting may also suggest the opposite: that the women has just composed the letter and is reticently handing it over to be sent. Regardless, the viewers are not permitted to know the contents of the letter; we can only make assumptions based on the details of the scene that may come together as any number of epistolary circumstances.[1] There is certainly a story

---

[1] Alpers, *The Art of Describing*, p. 142.

Figure 1 Johannes Vermeer, 'The Love Letter' (*c*.1669–70), Rijksmuseum

here, but the curiousness of the image does not settle onto one interpretation alone.[2]

It was during the early modern period, the time of Vermeer's painting, that the groundwork for modern postal services was established, particularly in nations with distant territories that depended on timely correspondence for trade and economic prosperity.[3] The colonial expansion of such maritime powers as the Venetian, British, and Dutch empires made commercial and diplomatic

---

[2] Alpers, *The Art of Describing*, p. 196. 'The pictures depict the form that social intercourse took but serve as a device that permits the Dutch artist to avoid its narrative dimensions.'
[3] See Campbell-Smith, *Masters of the Post* and Garfield, *To the Letter*.

correspondence indispensable and, as a consequence, created the channels by which private correspondence too became ubiquitous in the domestic sphere.[4] Letters, amorous or otherwise, are especially prominent in Dutch painting at about mid century. The domestic scenes of Gerard ter Borch (1617–81) and Johannes Vermeer (1632–75) very often depict people, women especially, writing letters and reading them, with various others there to hear and overhear their contents. Musical instruments, recently played, are very often nearby in these paintings, as symbols of domesticity perhaps, but also of transience and the exchange of voices over distances great and small.

One rather devastating painting by Pieter Codde (1599–1678), 'A lady seated at a virginal holding a letter', depicts a woman in a black silk dress with her back turned to the viewer, seated at a virginal.[5] Her head is lowered towards the keyboard and her gleaming pearl earrings are just visible. Her right arm hangs listlessly by her side, while the other rests on the back of a chair, turned in front of the instrument. In her right hand is a recently read letter and nearby is a viola da gamba that leans against the table. The unsettling scene implies that her mournful gesture has something to do with the letter's contents, which are unknown to the viewer. The two musical instruments do not merely imply that music-making might occur in this space; the letter creates a discord because the viola da gamba remains, perhaps permanently, without a player. Countless other paintings of the period give similarly intriguing glimpses into the daily lives of men and women and unite, in mysteriously compelling ways, letters with music.

Although epistolary communication fundamentally involves two parties – the writer and the recipient – letter paintings of early modernity tacitly serve to create a third perspective: that of the viewer, which complements and complicates the nature of the communication. Vermeer's paintings depict scenes of private intercourse, and letters may be assumed to contain the most private and revealing of thoughts. But letters were seldom private matters. The significance of music in these paintings is no doubt symbolic of voices exchanged in the absence of the other, but it may also be practical if, as this study shows, letters could themselves be sung to accompanying music. Not only was there a rich tradition of letter-writing manuals printed in Dutch during the seventeenth century, the poetic trope of the *Dichtbrief* – poetic letters – seems to have run in tandem with it.[6] The connection between music and letters is perhaps literal

---

[4] Alpers, *The Art of Describing*, p. 197.
[5] The painting is in a private collection; an image of it can be found on the Christie's listing found here: www.christies.com/en/lot/lot-4684697. See also Sutton, Vergara, and Jensen Adams, *Love Letters*, pp. 84–85.
[6] See Sutton, Vergara, and Jensen Adams, *Love Letters*, pp. 27–41.

as well as symbolic. The cittern in Vermeer's painting has more to do with the letter than one might initially assume. Letters themselves, though seemingly silent, were also musical.

What Is a Musical Love Letter?

The musical love letter, or *lettera amorosa*, was a distinct subgenre of secular vocal music in the late sixteenth and seventeenth centuries. It coincided with the increase in personal epistolary exchange during this period. Its roots however extend back to antiquity, both in its form as poetry rather than prose and in its conspicuous play on representational ambiguity (see Section 1). The *lettera amorosa* transforms epistolary communication into a public performance. Not only does it deliberately confuse the *personae* of writer and recipient – who is it that performs the letter? – it also places the listener in an unusual position. Like the viewer of Vermeer's painting, the listener of a *lettera amorosa* is somehow implicated in the scene.

It is perhaps not surprising that the *lettera amorosa* is difficult to define. The musical performance of epistolary poetry by way of improvisation may have begun many centuries before the genre was circumscribed. Even after the first instances of notated musical letters at the turn of the sixteenth century, the large stylistic, textural, and formal variety of the genre suggests no clear musical parameters by which to define it. The epistolary cantatas of the mid eighteenth century are for instance a far cry from the *frottole* of the early 1500s (see Sections 5 and 2). Even the poetry itself, although epistolary in some way, betrays widely different approaches to style and signification. To make matters worse, or better depending on one's perspective, the history of *lettere amorose* seems to run parallel to the mangled story of the term *rappresentativo* when applied to music. The famous love letters of Claudio Monteverdi were given the designation *in genere rappresentativo* ('in the representative genre') but there is no consensus, historical or contemporary, on what that is supposed to mean.[7]

A consistent definition for or application of such terms is perhaps less important than the conceptual and performative issues that such a debate raises. To understand the conceptual underpinnings of the *lettera amorosa* is to see it as a mode of musical expression in which representation itself is the subject. The 'representative' genre is one in which time, place, and perspective are deliberately ambiguous.

The term *stile rappresentativo* originates in the theories of the most famous musical academy of the late sixteenth century: the Florentine Camerata. Pietro de'

---

[7] There has been significant scholarly interest in issues of voice and representation in musicological studies focused on Italian secular music; see, for example, Carter, 'Beyond Drama', 1–46; Calcagno, *From Madrigal to Opera*; Murata, 'Image and Eloquence', pp. 411–22. See also Tim Carter's *Monteverdi's Voices*.

Bardi, son of the Camerata's noble patron Giovanni de' Bardi, wrote that 'il canto in istile rappresentativo' was first proposed by Vincenzo Galilei (1520–91), the accomplished composer, music theorist, and father of Galileo Galilei.[8] The *stile rappresentativo* is sometimes translated as 'the theatrical style', though there is no scholarly consensus about how it should be defined. This concept seems to be closely related to the Camerata's most influential contribution – recitative or *stile recitativo* – a musically heighted oratory, somewhere between speech and song, in which the natural inflections of a text were conveyed by a melody. This is of course the basis for Florence's greatest musical invention of the period: opera.[9] Confusingly, the term was used to denote theatre music, music for solo voice in the recitative style, five-voice polyphony, or, even more nebulous, music that represents something, usually a text, in a particularly dramatic or expressive way. If the *stile rappresentativo* was not really a style at all, why call it one? Musicians of the early seventeenth century, notably the theorist Giovanni Battista Doni (1595–1647) and even Claudio Monteverdi (1567–1643), insisted that 'rappresentativo' was in fact a special category of music, that it used the magical properties of melody to represent human emotion to the greatest degree of vividness and immediacy. Through Monteverdi, the term was associated with this curious subgenre of Italian secular vocal music at the turn of the seventeenth century: the *lettera amorosa*.

As mentioned, there is no clear stylistic unity in the repertory of epistolary music examined here. Monteverdi's love letters are lengthy pieces for solo voice in a declamatory style, whereas *lettere* by others are madrigals for several voices, duets, and other *concertato* pieces (see Section 2). In his *Trattato della music scenica* of 1633–5, Doni's valiant effort to distinguish three musical styles – *recitativo*, *rappresentativo*, and *espressivo* – illustrates a fundamental problem: some of the characteristics he uses to define these terms have to do with musical technique, others concern the theatrical *mise-en-scène*, and still others have more to do with delivery than anything inherent to the composition itself. In a passage from the eleventh chapter, he writes:

> But for 'representative', we should understand that kind of melody which is truly proportionate to the stage, that is, for every kind of dramatic action that one wishes to represent (the Greeks say μιμεῖσθαι imitate) in song. ... Therefore it pleases me better to call this style accommodated to the stage

---

[8] From Pietro de' Bardi's letter to Giovan Battista Doni; see Strunk, *Source Readings in Music History*, pp. 15–17.
[9] The practice of musical recitative was for the Florentines a revival of singing practices from antiquity. It was a way to recapture the transformative power of the ancient Greek modes that were said to have powerful ethical and moral consequences for listeners.

rappresentativo or *scenico*, rather than *recitativo*, because the actors ... did not recite but represent the actions and human manners.[10]

The representative or theatrical style seems, quite logically, to be music appropriate for the stage and for imitating as opposed to narrating action. It will not come as a surprise then that the earliest example of the term can be found on the title page of Guilio Caccini's opera *L'Euridice* of 1600. The slightly later but quintessential example of music composed in this style was, supposedly, Claudio Monteverdi's opera *L'Arianna*, performed in 1608 in Mantua for festivities following the wedding of Francesco Gonzaga and Margherita of Savoy.[11]

Unfortunately, most musical pieces bearing this title have little to do with opera, and many have a tenuous connection to staged drama, if at all. The situation with letters is particularly complex, since they seem to sit at a juncture between performing contexts, artistic media, and interpretive strategies. In a print from 1623, Monteverdi published Arianna's lament alongside two madrigals that had originally appeared in his 1619 Seventh Book of madrigals: these are given as 'due lettere amorose in genere rappresentativo' ('two love letters in the representative genre'). The distinction between style and genre may be telling, but its consequences are by no means obvious. As Section 3 illustrates, the texts of love letters *in genere rappresentativo* are similar to operatic laments in their subject matter, musical disposition, and psychological pacing, but *lettere amorose* exploit the vividness and emotional potency of the *genere rappresentativo* to a non-dramatic end: they reorient the lamenting lover towards stylized perspectival play.

Doni's interest in the *stile rappresentativo* can be explained in part because it is, supposedly, a special category of that great Florentine development: the *stile recitativo*. Despite its oblique relationship to the theatre, *rappresentativo* is often seen as a particularly emotive class of music for solo voice and continuo in the recitative style: the affections of one person represented in a verisimilar manner by one singer. Monteverdi's love letters – and those of several other seventeenth-century composers – are in fact written in affective recitative that, in many cases, is used to embody or represent the emotions of a particular person (see Section 4). Later in his treatise Doni employs

---

[10] 'Ma per Rappresentativa intendere debbiamo quella sorte di melodìa, che è veramente proporzionata alla Scena, cioè per ogni sorte di azione Dramatica, che si voglia rappresentare (i Greci dicono μιμεῖσθαι imitare) col canto, che è quasi l'istesso, che l'odierno stile Recitativo, e non del tutto medesimo ... Più dunque mi piace di chiamare questo stile accomodato alle Scene, Rappresentativo, o Scenico, che Recitativo; sì perché gli Attori ... non recitano, ma rappresentano; imitando le azioni, e costume umani.' Doni, *Trattato della musica scenica* (1633–5), cap. XI, p. 30, *Lyra Barberina* (1763), ii; trans. Carter, in Fabbri, *Monteverdi*, pp. 166–67.

[11] Monteverdi wrote to Alessandro Striggio in 1620 about Arianna being in the 'genere di canto rappresentativo' (Venice, 4 April 1620; L. 53).

a different strategy. He defines 'rappresentativo' not by some purely musical characteristic, which does not really work, but instead bases his classification on the type of poetry:

> Those who 'recite' are only those who utter narrative poetry (that is, in which the poet speaks in his own voice without introducing other characters) ... but not in imitations, in which the poet's own voice does not appear, but instead the represented characters speak directly, like in dramas ... since, as I said above, this is not really reciting, or recounting; but representing or imitating.[12]

Doni seems to acknowledge that we do not need to have a coherent plot to represent the speech and actions of characters musically; the indispensable element is rather a singer embodying a character instead of narrating action. However, the central conceit of musical love letters is that the performer may not be 'speaking' in their own voice, but that they may actually be relating the words of another person to an audience who knows only part of the story. Indeed, this is precisely why Doni criticized Monteverdi's *lettera amorosa* 'Se i languidi miei sguardi' for being a piece for soprano on a text clearly written from the male perspective. While letters may 'speak', they almost never speak for themselves. Any attempt to define the term 'rappresentativo' through poetic mode – as mimesis and not diegesis – is ineffective not only for the *lettera amorosa* but also for probably the most famous piece to bear this designation. Monteverdi's *Combattimento di Tancredi e Clorinda* from his Eighth Book (1638) is a madrigal in *genere rappresentativo* that sets poetry in the epic mode, and thus comprises text almost entirely in narrative.[13]

As far as musical love letters are concerned, *rappresentativo* is not really a style but rather a mode, a manner, a genre – *genere rappresentativo* – that transcends technique and spills over into the realm of performance and

---

[12] 'Perciocchè recitano solo quelli, che proferiscono Poesìe narrative (che sono quelle, nelle quali parla sempre il Poeta in persona sua, senza introdurre altri, che favellino, come Lucrezio nel suo Poema) o al più le miste (quali sono i Poemi eroici, e Romanzi, l'Eneide, la Gerusalemme, il Furioso &c. dove alcuna volta parla il Poeta, e spesso anco introduce altri a favellare) e non già imitazioni, nelle quali non apparisce la persona del Poeta; ma direttamente parlano i personaggi rappresentati, come in tutte i Drami, e in questi Dialoghetti, che hanno introdotto; e per la maggior parte nell'Egloghe di Vergilio, e di Teocrito: imperocchè, come io diceva di sopra, ciò non è veramente recitare, o raccontare; ma rappresentare, o imitare.' Doni, *Trattato della musica scenica*, cap. XII, pp. 31–32.

[13] It may seem less surprising, then, that in 1608 Aquilino Coppini used the term to describe five-voice madrigals: 'The representative music [*musica rappresentativa*] of Signor Monteverdi's Fifth Book of madrigals, governed by the natural expression of the human voice in moving the affections, stealing into the ear in the sweetest manner and thereby making itself the most pleasant tyrant of souls, is indeed worthy of being sung and heard.' Coppini, *Il secondo libro della musica di Claudio Monteverdi ... fatta spirituale*; transcribed by E. Vogel; trans. Carter in Fabbri, *Monteverdi*, p. 105.

psychology. Similarly, the epistolary 'mode' of the musical *lettera amorosa* is distinguished by its complex performativity and the way it implicates different perspectives in representational ambiguity. The *genere rappresentativo* is entirely appropriate for the *lettera amorosa* not because it tends to be emotionally charged recitative, but because it is, musically, poetically, and performatively, a representational conundrum. The closest Doni gets to capturing this fascinating nexus of words, tones, and delivery is in the *Annotazioni* to his musical compendium which he compiled 'per amore de gl'Idioti' finally to clarify what he means by *rappresentativo*, now given as a synonym for *espressivo*:[14]

> *Espressiva* [*rappresentativa*][15] then endeavours to express the affections; and in some places those natural accents of emotive speech: and it is this that has the greatest power over the human soul since, when it is accompanied by vivid actions, and by a speech proportionate to the subject, it marvellously provokes smiles, tears, distain, etc.[16]

---

[14] Doni had made a tripartite classification between *recitativo*, *espressivo*, and *rappresentativo* but here the latter two are conflated and the types of recitative (which he also calls 'lo stile monodico') are re-classified as *narrativo*, *speciale recitativo*, and *espressivo*.

[15] Doni, *Annotazioni sopra il compendio de' generi, e de' modi della musica*, p. 60; 'l'Espressivo, che altri dicono Rappresentativo'.

[16] Doni, *Annotazioni sopra il compendio de' generi, e de' modi della musica*, pp. 61–62; 'Nell'Espressiva dunque si fa professione di bene esprimere gli affetti; & in qualche parte quegl'accenti naturali del parlare patetico: e questa è quella ch'hà grandissima forza ne gl'animi humani: a segno che, quando è accompagnata d'una vivace attione, e d'un parlare proportionato al soggetto, maravigliosamente commuove il riso, il pianto, lo sdegno, &c.'

1 Voices of Antiquity

The answer to your question is that nothing is more useful than this art that has no usefulness.[17]
—Ovid

In a comedy by Antiphanes from the fourth century BCE the poet Sappho begins with a riddle. 'What creature is it', she asks her companions, 'that is female in nature and hides in its womb unborn children who, although they are voiceless, speak to people far away?'[18] When no one provides the correct response, Sappho answers the riddle herself: the creature is a letter. Its children – the alphabetic letters contained within – remain silent to those close by and yet communicate with those who are distant.[19] Sappho's riddle suggests that letters can be paradoxes of communication. They 'speak' and yet their words seem to defy both physical distance and sensory medium. They belong, presumably, to the writer but depend on a reader. Lying at the heart of Sappho's riddle is the curious suggestion that orality, or, more specifically, vocality, is both inherently absent from and necessarily present in epistolary communication. The writer in this case effectively 'borrows' the voice of the reader, while the reader 'hears' that of the writer. Although more recent times, our own perhaps more than ever, have given almost exclusive rights to silent reading, letters – in all their various forms – reveal that the historical predominance of reading aloud was not merely a matter of practicality or convenience. The performance of letters, their transformation from something seen to something heard, had remarkable consequences for the way they mediated human connections.

The diversity of epistolary genres – from actual correspondence, through fictional letters, to epistolary novels – testifies to the intricate and reciprocal channels of communication that letters could create. Letters did not simply convey practical information, although that was certainly one of their functions. The history of letters, love letters in particular, is also one of ambiguity,

---

[17] 'Cum bene quaesieris quid agam, magis utile nil est artibus his, quae nil utilitatis habent'. From Ovid's letter to his friend Aurelius Cotta Maximus Massalinus (*Epistulae ex Ponto*, I. V. 53–54), quoted and translated in Ordine, *The Usefulness of the Useless*, p. 47. See also Ovid, *Epistulae ex Ponto, Book 1*, pp. 70–71.

[18] Sappho, Kassel–Austen fr. 194; trans. in Carson, *Eros the Bittersweet*, p. 98; alternative translation in *Fragmenta Comica* (Göttingen, 2021), pp. 12–13. See also Rosenmeyer, *Ancient Epistolary Fictions*, p. 96.

[19] 'The female creature is the letter (epistle). The unborn children are the letters (of the alphabet) it carries. And the letters, although they have no voices, speak to people far away, whomever they wish. But if some other person happens to be standing right beside the one who is reading, he will not hear'; trans. Carson, *Eros the Bittersweet*, pp. 96–97.

performativity, and even musicality. A personal letter in the twenty-first century may, upon initial consideration, appear as a relic of the past: a form of communication that was once ubiquitous but is now, for most intents and purposes, dead as a doornail. There may have been a time when emails were simply letters in electronic format, and text messages voicemails transcribed, but it did not take long for what was simply a method of transmission – electronic versus physical – to alter fundamentally the mode of expression.

Still, some have pushed back against the narrative that letters, paper correspondence, and mails, in general, are in terminal decline. Sociologist Liz Stanley has argued that while new technologies have perennially transformed the mechanisms of communication, a certain 'letterness' in written communications curiously endures, what she calls 'epistolary intent'.[20] For many historians, letters are still the primary windows into the activities of men and women of the past, and their obsolescence as a medium somehow makes them even more seductive. Without a clear practical function, letters can be romanticized simply as beautiful vestiges of a time wholly distant and unfamiliar. But their complicated relationship to time, place, and identity may help to explain their appeal and unwillingness to die completely. To write them now is to isolate and revel in their aesthetic facets, or to find the usefulness of the useless. This idea was one Nuccio Ordine found enduring in the work of artists and thinkers from Ovid to Victor Hugo.[21]

Letters, especially personal or amorous ones, involve a particular kind of distillation of the human experience. Unlike telephone calls or text messages which hold the promise of real-time communication, letters are more overtly mediated. They contain a kind of humanized synthesis of information that is by definition 'out of time' and sent to someone who is not there. They can provide biased accounts, analyses of emotions, and relate past events to present thoughts through the filter of hindsight. Letters tell stories of actions and reactions to events which may have changed over time and allow the past to simmer cerebrally with the present until the two are potentially indistinguishable. The early modern period, during which literacy rates began modestly to increase, witnessed the publication of countless manuals on letter writing, including detailed instructions on modes of address, practical conventions, and rhetorical strategies.[22] This should hardly come as a surprise considering that written

---

[20] Stanley, 'The Death of the Letter?' pp. 240–54. Stanley defines epistolary intent as something 'which involves the intention to communicate, in writing or a cognate representational medium, to another person who is "not there" because removed in time/space from the writer, and doing so with the hope or expectation of a response', p. 242.

[21] Ordine points out passages from such authors as Ovid (quoted at the outset of this section), Dante, Kant, Hugo, and David Foster Wallace, all of which find that utilitarian 'usefulness' is the surest poison for artistic expression.

[22] See Jensen, *Writing Love* and Kong, *Lettering the Self in Medieval and Early Modern France*.

communications were at the time indispensable methods for conducting business, diplomacy, and personal affairs. What is surprising is the way in which letters and epistles have always had a place outside the realm of pure practicality – since antiquity artists and writers have written letters not merely as useful tools for correspondence, but as fictions, poems, paintings, and, most relevant here, pieces of music. Although we might be tempted to assume that art letters appreciated solely for their useless beauty could only exist in a world in which they have no large-scale practical function (i.e., our own), their history tells a rather different story. Is there usefulness in a 'useless' letter? Yes, in the remarkable way letters can represent the contradictions of human experience.

What, then, is the relationship between a letter for practical epistolary communication and one stylized into poetry or prose fiction? In her work on eros in ancient Greek literature, Anne Carson writes that the power of fictional letters, in poems as in dramas, resides in their aptness to express the bittersweetness of love. 'Letters are the mechanism of erotic paradox', she writes, 'at once connective and separative, painful and sweet. Letters construct the space of desire and kindle it in those contradictory emotions that keep the lover alert to his own impasse'.[23] A love letter vivifies the mechanisms of eros by having 'simulacra of presence'.[24] It represents the desire to overcome place (by creating presence from absence), surpass distance (by making the near far and the far near), and, perhaps most profoundly, control time (by collapsing the past onto the present).[25] But what happens when a letter is not merely read, but set to music? To what purpose do the useful and useless collide when a letter is sung as a musical piece? There is something about a *sung* letter that takes its erotic peculiarities even further. By amplifying, so to speak, the contents of a letter, musical performance reverses the process by which letters tend to keep their secrets unrevealed. Lovers often write down what cannot, for various reasons, be said aloud. In what is surely one of the most extraordinary literary love letters, in Jane Austen's final novel *Persuasion* (1817), Captain Wentworth inscribes his soul into a letter which he writes while seated not two feet from his beloved Anne. And yet, music can have those secret sentiments resound for all to hear.

The *lettera amorosa* creates a unique dynamic between text and music that both heightens and complicates the erotic paradoxes embodied by the epistolary poem. It interacts with the amorous ambiguities already present in the text but, by virtue of it being performed, creates some of its own as well. It is a sounded enactment of that which may be, for various reasons, forbidden. If the epistolary genre served to transform, or, to echo Claudio Achillini's *lettera* set by Claudio

---

[23] Carson, *Eros the Bittersweet*, p. 92.   [24] Stanley, 'The Death of the Letter?' p. 244.
[25] Carson, *Eros the Bittersweet*, p. 111. 'A desire to bring the absent into presence, or to collapse far and near, is also a desire to foreclose then upon now'.

Monteverdi, to 'distill' the lover's thoughts and emotions into verse, then the music which set it was an equally transformative medium. One may reasonably assume that a love letter sung aloud is one of many early modern aesthetic conceits, a kind of aural version of the literary voyeurism that pervades some genres of seventeenth-century art. There is no doubt that love letters as solo songs and ensemble pieces participate in the period's love of the impractical and stylized, particularly in Italy. What should be added to this, however, is an acknowledgement that the vocal complexities of *lettere amorose* are also vestiges of this tradition of antiquity, in which the force of writing was largely dependent on whether the words were said aloud. As the poetry of *lettere amorose* reveals, the veracity of the contents of a letter – which told of desire as often as it accused of infidelity – seems to be ratified and made true, even if it is not, by the voice of the performer. This is particularly the case if the singer is meant to 'stand in' as the reader and recipient. The letter thus becomes a kind of oral contract which both reflects and unites mythology with legal history.

There are many ways in which music can transform a poem. In the case of epistles, two primary mechanisms stand out: the first is sensory, in which the tactile, aural, and visual converge; and the second is perspectival, in which voices and their addressees are commandeered in the name of love. A musical setting, then, transforms a letter in a manner that is both sensory (because it oscillates between seen and heard) and perspectival (because it plays with a voice that belongs to one but is performed by another). Music can control time, space, and identity by commandeering a singing voice to recreate a desired but fictional immediacy and intimacy. In music, controlling time is tantamount to controlling reality. Finally, a musical epistle can enact, by way of its listeners, the triangulation that Carson finds indispensable for the eroticism of letters in Greek and Roman antiquity. In the exchange of *lettere amorose* there are not merely two actors – the writer and the recipient – but also a third perspective belonging to one who figuratively reads, or rather listens, over the shoulder. In complicating a situation that implies two interlocutors, music can conjure 'a third person who is not literally there, making suddenly visible the difference between what is ... and what could be'.[26] In many epistolary poems from the seventeenth century the supposed dichotomy between reader and writer is further complicated by the added perspective of the letter itself, which, as the poetic 'I', takes on its own persona. In a musical performance, the letter becomes a kind of messenger for the words of the writer and 'speaks', albeit ambiguously, through the voice of the singer. This kind of perspectival triangulation endured to marvellous effect in painting of that period; by navigating the

---

[26] Carson, *Eros the Bittersweet*, p. 111.

web of mirrors and reflections in a picture like Velázquez's *Las Meninas*, viewers are surprised to find themselves implicated in the scene, their own position equally unfixed as those of the painted characters (Figure 2).

The early history of musical letters is extensive and spans several centuries and genres.[27] Nearly all the musical scholarship on the topic of the *lettera amorosa* has been centred on or oriented towards the love letters of Claudio Monteverdi. But the *lettere amorose* of the seventeenth century were neither the beginning nor the end of this rich tradition of singing letters. The provocative

Figure 2 Diego Velázquez, 'Las Meninas' (1656), Museo del Prado

---

[27] No less important, though not discussed here, is the rich medieval literary tradition of fictional letters. This includes, amongst others, those of fourteenth-century poet and composer Guillaume de Machaut (*c.* 1300–77) and his infamous *Le livre dou voir dit* (the *Voir dit*) written in the years 1363–65.

monodic *lettere amorose* of the early seventeenth century have a musical and literary context in sung epistles of antiquity, and love letters were transformed through the later cantata repertory of the seventeenth and eighteenth centuries.

Although studies in the history of literature and classics seldom deal directly with the musical afterlives of love letters, they do reveal that performativity and orality was central to their paradoxical nature. I propose that early modern musical settings of love letters rekindled a complex kind of vocality which was rooted in the letters of antiquity and endured, despite the increased prominence of silent reading, in the peculiar musical genre of the *lettera amorosa*.[28] In the love letter, as in the musical genres in which it flourished, a composer did not merely set a poem by matching image to affect and character to voice. Just as a letter may be read (i.e., interpreted) by its recipient, music can likewise 'read' a poem and, by consequence, transform it.

The Greek treatise *On Style*, attributed to Demetrius and possibly composed in the second century BCE, characterizes letters as iconic reflections of their writers: 'everyone writes a letter in the virtual image [*eikōn*] of his own soul'.[29] This idea that letters send forth not just the words and thoughts of the writer, but some tangible and perceptible trace of themselves was a compelling one. In his *Epistles*, Seneca the Younger writes to Lucilius about how a letter is the most pleasurable of all 'images' of absent friends, for letters, in the manner of moving and breathing pictures, 'brings real traces':

> If the pictures of your absent friends are pleasing to us, though they only refresh the memory and lighten our longing by a solace that is unreal and unsubstantial, how much more pleasant is a letter, which brings real traces.[30]

The same passage was paraphrased centuries later in an emblem book by the Dutch artist and humanist Otto van Veen, published in Antwerp as *Amorum emblemata* (1608).[31] The love-letter motto, *litteris absentes videmus* ('we see absent people through letters'), is accompanied by short texts that meditate on how letters make it possible to see and hear absent lovers (Figure 3). The passage from Seneca is paired with one attributed to Cicero, along with brief poems in Dutch and French.[32] Van Veen makes a telling change to Seneca's

---

[28] See Kivy, *The Performance of Reading*.

[29] Demetrius, *On Style*, in Aristotle, Longinus, Demetrius, *Poetics. Longinus: On the Sublime. Demetrius: On Style*, Loeb Classical Library 199, 227, pp. 479–81.

[30] 'Si imagines nobis amicorum absentium iucundae sunt, quae memoriam renovant et desiderium falso atque inani solacio levant, quanto iucundiores sunt litterae, quae vera amici absentis vestigia, veras notas adferunt?' Seneca the Younger, *Epistles, Volume I*, pp. 262–65.

[31] Van Veen was also a draughtsman and a humanist, suggested both the classical quotations in his emblem books, and the fact that he often used a Latinized name Octavio (or Otho) Vaenius.

[32] Some versions of the 1608 print omit the poem in Dutch and substitute it with one in Italian ('Congiunto sempre'); a copy now in the Rubenstein Library at Duke University (N7740.V345 1608) also has curious half page inserts which includes poems in Spanish.

EMBLEMATA

Cic. LITTERIS ABSENTES VIDEMUS.

*Vivis in extremis ignoti partibus orbis,
Et procul ex oculis datis amica meis.
At te præsentem, absentem licèt, esse putabo,
Si mihi sit verbis charta notatuis.*

Senec. Si imagines amantibus, etiam absentium, iucundæ sunt, quod memoriam renouent, & desiderium absentiæ fallo atque inani solatio leuent: quantò iucundiores sunt litteræ, quæ vera amantis vestigia, veras notas afferunt.

Door brieven kreught.

Door misdaet ban tostsiche en sorte infinite bjeuren,
Hoe berre bupten afsonderp / min siet en bpreche sijn lief,
Cupido sterchpten bani altsen om sijnss gheriet.
En minuetticn lpdesstinder tgheit der afselsteun.

La lettre perle.

L'Amour impatient de toute longue absence,
Inuenta le moyen pour le joindre d'abord,
Oues quablent de corps, par un papier escris,
A quel il peut le mal, qui sa poictrine eslance.

FLAM.

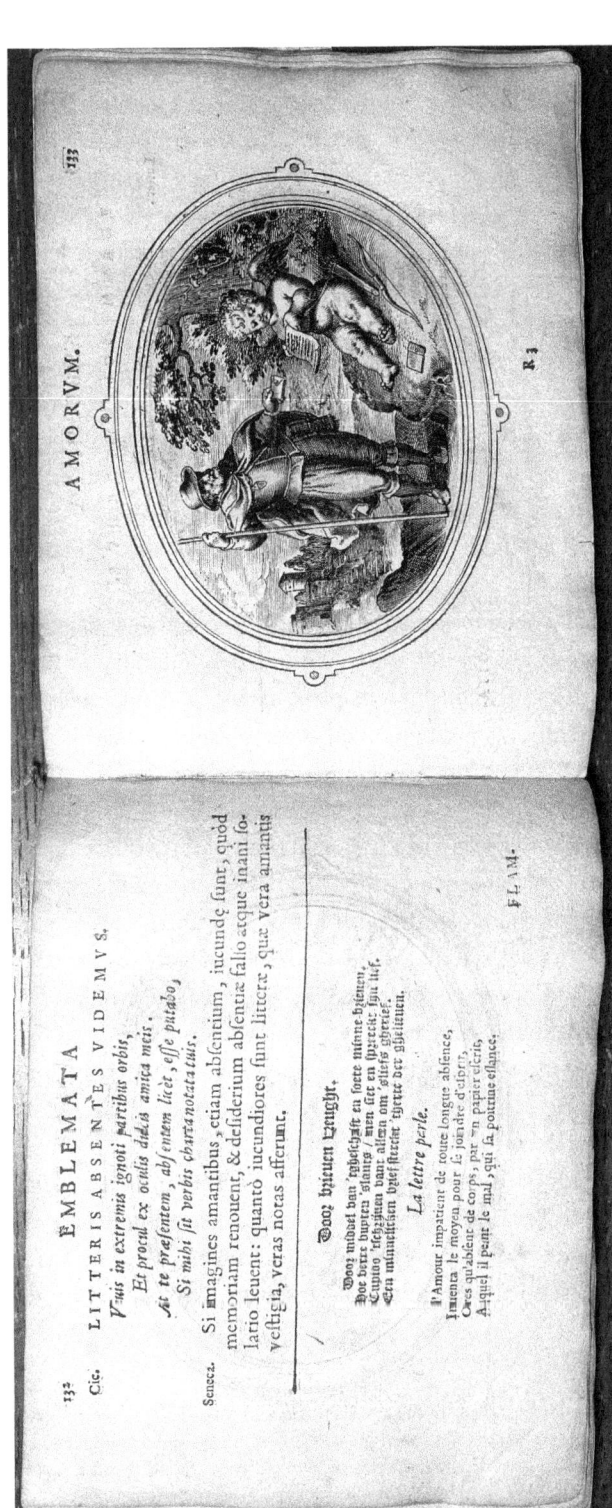

AMORVM.

Figure 3 Otto van Veen, *Amorum emblemata* (Antwerp, 1608), pp. 132–33, David M. Rubenstein Rare Book and Manuscript Library, Duke University.

phrase in replacing 'imagines nobis *amicorum*' with 'imagines *amantibus*', swapping images of friends for those of lovers. In van Veen's emblem, which shows a messenger delivering a letter to Cupid, it is the vestiges of a lover that a letter brings ('quae vera amantis vestigia'), and the traces are the notes on the page ('veras notas afferunt'). The visual and sensorial imagery of van Veen's emblem actualize the ways in which friends and lovers imagine their letters fulfilling their desires. Lovers are separated by both distance and time but may overcome both if they use words to recreate absent ones. In writing as in reading, lovers may see and hear their beloved, and in turn, be seen and heard in return.

Just as van Veen's emblems encourage readers to 'see' their lovers in letters, a musical setting likewise realizes the desire to imagine both speaking and listening to them. As the French verse accompanying van Veen's emblem suggests, the letter can speak – 'la lettre parle' – *to* the beloved, but also *as* the beloved, depending on one's perspective.[33] While a letter is abstractly a form of speech, it can only function as such if it is no longer subject to the immediacy, the real-time temporality, of actual conversation; letters and their responses are, by definition, separated by intervals of time. Many texts of poetic love letters refer to pens, paper, and ink, likewise casting the words as explicitly written, even as they aspire to speak. The conceit of the sung letter is therefore that it presents atemporal words through a temporal medium. The result is similar to what Roland Barthes described as being 'wedged between two tenses'; in a fragment from *A Lover's Discourse*, he writes that the beloved's absence distorts the perception of the present moment, a tense which is the most 'difficult', 'insupportable', and 'a pure portion of anxiety'.[34] And yet in a *lettera amorosa* the listener is required to meditate in the present tense, wedged not only between two tenses but two senses as well. Music makes tangible the lover's impossible imagining – that the letter speaks – by giving words that are explicitly seen through a medium that is explicitly heard.

In realizing the sensory transformations of poetic love letters, music therefore provides a means by which the manipulation of time actually mimics the feeling of being in love. 'And love is an issue of control', Carson writes, but 'what does it mean to control another human being? to control oneself?'.[35] Once again, a singing voice can be used to transform the perspectives embedded in and

---

[33] Van Veen, *Amorum emblemata*, p. 132.

[34] 'This singular distortion generates a kind of insupportable present; I am wedged between two tenses, that of the reference and that of the allocution: You have gone (which I lament), you are here (since I am addressing you). Whereupon I know what the present, that difficult tense, is: A pure portion of anxiety'; Barthes, *A Lover's Discourse*, p. 15.

[35] Carson, *Eros the Bittersweet*, pp. 121–22.

implied by the text; it represents the act of taking control and relinquishing it at the same time. In his discussion of a *ballata* from Dante's *Vita nuova*, a poem that is itself crafted as a kind of love letter, Martin Eisner writes: 'the problem is this: how can the poem be both the words Dante speaks and the addressee of these words?'[36] The answer is that it can, especially if it is sung as a musical piece, as was the case for Dante's *ballata* set to music in an English translation by Dante Gabriel Rossetti.[37] The mythological love letters of antiquity further suggest that the words of one read aloud by another could be binding, almost contractual, as they are in the story of Acontius and Cydippe recounted in Ovid's *Heroides*.

Love letters allow their authors to circumvent the obstacles of time and place, as we have seen, but also effectively to rewrite reality. Letters, as 'issues' of love, seek to exert control over amorous desire, to weave a kind of alternate reality and, in some cases, coerce the recipient into validating it. 'If I write my desires and you read them aloud then your voice makes it so', some of these poems seem to imply. If a letter can use words to freeze the image of the beloved as crafted by the writer, then music allows the singer (the recipient, perhaps) to thaw it, so to speak, and remould it according to their own emotional reaction. To paraphrase Eisner, the poem may make the animate inanimate in becoming an amorous epistle, but music reverses this process: it reanimates the inanimate and, consequently, blends senses with perspectives.[38]

What then is the nature of this epistolary vocality inherited from antiquity and how might it be translated into the poetry and music of early modernity? In her study of Ovidian erotics, Victoria Rimell remarks that a distinguishing strategy in Ovid's works on love is the use of a syntax that artfully confounds the subject of desire with its object.[39] The dynamics between lover and beloved, male and female, guilty and wronged are deliberately unstable. Ovid makes exemplary use, Rimell writes, 'of the potential disjointedness of the elegiac couplet to jigsaw together emotions, sexualities, and genders'.[40] In the third book of the *Ars amatoria*, Ovid counsels his women readers to 'look at him who looks at you, send back his charming smile' ('spectantem specta, ridenti mollia ride').[41] The reflective imagery is not merely a tool for amorous reciprocation: it confuses who is looking at whom and calls the lovers' respective positions into question. In the ancient world, mirrors were highly paradoxical: 'they give women the power to know and control appearances, but in doing so expose the

---

[36] The reference is to Dante's poem 'Ballata, i' voi che tu ritrovi Amore' from the *Vita nuova*; see Eisner, *Dante's New Life of the Book*, p. 73.

[37] In Dante, *The New Life*; see Eisner, *Dante's New Life of the Book*, p. 66.

[38] Eisner, *Dante's New Life of the Book*, p. 75.   [39] Rimell, *Ovid's Lovers*, p. 82.

[40] Rimell, *Ovid's Lovers*, p. 154.

[41] The passage is found in Book 3 (513) of *Ars Amatoria* see Ovid, *Art of Love*, pp. 154–55. See also Rimell, *Ovid's Lovers*, p. 81.

limits of female individuation'.[42] Mirrors were the proxy by which Medusa and Narcissus saw their undoing, and letters – the 'image' of the writer's soul – were their literary analogues. In the *Heroides*, Ovid writes letters not just as the wronged women of mythology including Penelope, Dido, and Ariadne, but, in the latter part of the book, as the men who respond and receive responses in turn: Paris, Leander, and Acontius. The transformative power of reflections, in mirrors or in letters, permeates Ovid's writings on love. Whether they are read or heard, published or performed, letters have a seductive quality because they provide an oblique view of love. They allow for that third 'over the shoulder' perspective of Carson's eros since they are predicated on the idea that listeners may piece together the scene and imagine themselves as author or recipient. Anybody, as Rimell puts it, 'has the right to reply'.[43]

Many of the images evoked in the epistolary poems of later centuries can be traced to the letters of Ovid's *Heroides*, originally composed in Latin around the year 10 BCE. In the fifteenth letter, Sappho tells her lover, the boatman Phaon, that as she writes to him tears pour out of her eyes like drops of dew, blotting the paper in front of her: 'I write, and my eyes pour out tears ... just look how many blots there are just here!'[44] At the outset of her letter to Achilles in *Heroides* 3, Briseis likewise insists that these tears are not mere impediments to the legibility of her text, they are meaningful and communicative in and of themselves: 'whatever blots you see, her tears have made; but tears, too, have none the less the weight of words'.[45] The fact that Briseis writes of herself in the third person is significant also; like the letter itself the grammar creates another layer of distance that may, as we will see, have performative consequences. The blots (*liturae*) falling to leave stains on paper are poetically equated with the actual letters on the page, the 'notes' seen previously in van Veen's paraphrase of Seneca. The musical play on words from tears to blots to musical notes survives in Claudio Achillini's text for Monteverdi's *lettera amorosa* – 'leggete queste note' – in which the 'stains' are as much the lover's tears as they are inked noteheads. The letter is a tangible trace of the writer, tears are literally soaked into it, but it is also a mirror image of their soul. The reader may look into (i.e., read) that mirror and see their beloved but, at the same time, see a reflection of themselves. When in Monteverdi's *lettera* the singer utters Achillini's imperative to 'read these notes' they are doing just that, heeding the blots' command to see their lover as they see themselves.

---

[42] Rimell, *Ovid's Lovers*, p. 57.   [43] Rimell, *Ovid's Lovers*, p. 131.
[44] Ovid, *Heroides*, XV. 97–98, Sappho to Phaon, pp. 186–89. 'Scribimus, et lacrimis oculi rorantur obortis; | adspice, quam sit in hoc multa litura loco!' Note that the 'writer' is an authorial plural 'we' which suggests and image in which the eyes themselves (plural) are the ones doing the writing.
[45] Ovid, *Heroides*, III. 3–4, Briseis to Achilles, pp. 32–33. 'Quascumque adspicies, lacrimae fecere lituras; | sed tamen et lacrimae pondera vocis habent'.

At the turn of the seventeenth century, John Donne reimagined the idea of letters as mirrors in his own letter 'as' Sappho. The poem is written not to Phaon but, anachronistically, to the illusive Philaenis, a writer known only as the author of an ancient manual on sex.[46] In Donne's highly erotic text, Sappho looks upon herself as a mirror image of her female lover: 'likeness begets such strange self-flattery, | that touching myself, all seems done to thee'.[47] In these texts, the traces that letters bring – tears, reflections, notes – are seductively tangible. Readers are invited to meditate on the paper before them and see its qualities standing in for the physical attributes of its author. But music is, in performance at least, decidedly intangible. Its transience dissolves a letter into a fleeting moment, even as it too has a presence on the page written in the code of notation. It becomes, in other words, a literal manifestation of the wind that Sappho imagines carrying her words unreliably towards their destination. 'Do the zephyrs bear away my idly failing words?', she asks through Ovid's pen.[48]

The musicality of epistolary poetry in early modernity unites the images and expressive devices from both the Latin and Greek traditions. In his study of epigrams and inscriptions, Jesper Svenbro has likened the place of writing in ancient Greece to that of musical notation in the present. While it is certainly possible to read musical notation silently, more typical is for one to realize the notation in some way to hear what it means.[49] In musical notation as in epitaphs, visual signs directly interact with and imply their oral realization making them not only visual but acoustic signs as well. Verbs in the imperative have great importance in commemorative speech, in the way that such epigrammatic inscriptions seem to command readers to give voice to their words. Epitaphs from about the fifth century BCE, including the stele of Mnesitheos and others contemporary to it, instruct passersby to read out (*anáneimai*) and tell (*lége*) of the deceased for whom the votive monument was erected.[50] There is some overlap in nuance between Greek verbs used for reading and speaking in that they can also imply a kind of 'distribution' by way of voice. Likewise, as Svenbro has suggested, the verb *némein* (νέμειν) may also have meant 'to read' through its sense as 'to distribute, in the same way that *nómos* (νόμος) carried a musical definition meaning 'melody'. To read could also mean to sing

---

[46] Plant, ed. *Women Writers of Ancient Greece and Rome*, pp. 45–47.
[47] Donne, *The Complete English Poems*, p. 128.
[48] Ovid, *Heroides*, XV. 208, Sappho to Phaon, p. 195.
[49] Svenbro, *Phrasikleia*, p. 18. A more recent discussion is in Johnson, 'Toward a Sociology of Reading in Classical Antiquity', 593–627.
[50] The verb ἀνάνεμαι, *anáneimai* (read out) is given in the imperative in the stele of Mnesitheos of Aegina while λέγε, *lége* (tell) is found on an inscription on the plinth of a bronze statue (now lost) discovered at Halicarnassus. See Svenbro, *Phrasikleia*, pp. 48, 51, and 56, and Rawles, 'Simonides on Tombs, and the "Tomb of Simonides"', pp. 56–57.

in the sense that song is 'dispensed' or 'dispersed' by the voice just as words are.[51] This 'dispersion' carried a particular weight which could also be contractual: the Greek word *nómos* also means 'law', similar to the way the Latin *lex* ('law') is related to the verb *legere* ('to read').[52] In both cases to read is to utter aloud, and to utter aloud is a legally binding activity.

The mythological story of Cydippe and Acontius is a paradigmatic tale for the use of letters to exercise power over the voice of another (see Figure 4). The story survives in three primary sources, as discussed in detail by Patricia

Figure 4 Paulus Bor, 'Cydippe with the Apple of Acontius' (*c*.1645–55), Rijksmuseum

---

[51] Svenbro, *Phrasikleia*, pp. 111–12.
[52] As Svenbro points out, the etymological paths are not completely parallel, and it is only the Greek *némein* ('to read' or 'to distribute') that was used in a musical sense. See Svenbro, *Phrasikleia*, pp. 111–12.

Rosenmeyer in her study of ancient epistolary fictions.[53] The earliest is in *Aetia* by the Greek poet Callimachus and dates from the third century BCE, while the latter two are Latin: a set of epistles from Ovid's *Heroides* of the first century BCE, and the erotic prose letters of the late antique epistolographer Aristaenetus of the fifth century CE. The story is about Acontius, a young man from the island of Ceos, who falls immediately in love with Cydippe, an Athenian maiden, when the two meet during the festival of Apollo on the island of Delos. Eros inspires Acontius to pick up an apple and write a note to his new beloved. The mischievous god instructs the young man to carve this oath into the flesh of the apple: 'I swear by Artemis to marry Acontius'. He rolls the apple in front of Cydippe who picks it up and, out of curiosity, reads the inscription, unwittingly binding herself in marriage to Acontius. But Cydippe is already betrothed to another. Defeated, Acontius wanders through the woods continually carving the name of his beloved into the barks of trees.[54] Having unintentionally angered the goddess Artemis, Cydippe is repeatedly struck with a sudden illness the night before her intended nuptials, prompting her father to consult the Delphic oracle to explain the unfortunate events. Once the oracle reveals Cydippe's oath, the situation is resolved once Acontius and Cydippe marry and, presumably, live happily together.

In this story Eros instructs Acontius on how to use a letter to commit amorous fraud: his desire becomes Cydippe's words and her voice seals the marriage contract. The script belongs to Acontius but the consequences are for Cydippe. As Ovid writes in the first book of the *Ars Amatoria*, 'Cydippe was deceived by a letter written on a fruit, and was made the unwitting prisoner of her own words' (*Ars* 1.457–8).[55] The apple, as letter, gives way to the epistolary exchange between the unlikely lovers in *Heroides* 20 and 21. In his letter, Acontius points to Eros as the broker of the deceptive contract: 'Love was the lawyer that taught me knavery', he writes.[56] In her response, Cydippe admits that she was fearful even to see the words of Acontius's letter. While she read she made sure to keep silent 'without the slightest sound' so that her tongue would not again unwittingly swear some oath.[57] She likens both the letter and Acontius himself, whose name literally means javelin, to a dart that makes its injurious blow from a distance: 'you have the

---

[53] See Rosenmeyer, *Ancient Epistolary Fictions*, pp. 110–30.
[54] This would be recalled in Torquato Tasso's epic *Gerusalemme liberata* (1581) through the character of Erminia and later Nicea in the revised *Gerusalemme conquistata* (1593) in which the lovesick women carve the name of their beloved on the barks of trees.
[55] Ovid, *Art of Love,* pp. 44–45. Translation in Joseph Farrell, 'Reading and Writing the *Heroides*', 307–38 (p. 312).
[56] Ovid, *Heroides*, XX. 30, p. 277.
[57] Ovid, *Heroides*, XXI. 1–4, p. 293. See Rosenmeyer, *Ancient Epistolary Fictions*, p. 125.

keen point that deals wounds from afar … for I was pierced by your letter'.[58] The letter is a mirror image of its writer, and its force transcends distance and time. For Ovid, the love letter is 'a kind of psychosexual shibboleth'.[59] In the case of Acontius and Cydippe, the letter can be a deceptive but relatively safe tool for a man engaging in seduction. The stakes for the woman are considerably higher. For her, there are great risks in committing her feelings to paper.[60] Even the act of reading, in which another's words are voiced, can exact greater disclosure than she intends, transforming the letter into 'a document of incrimination'.[61] The tone, therefore, of poetic love letters written as or by women tends to be more sombre, particularly in the imitations of Ovid's *Heroides* from the sixteenth and seventeenth centuries. Vittoria Colonna's poetic epistle, 'Eccelso mio Signor, questa ti scrivo' – one of few such poems actually written by a woman – is modelled on Ovid's letter from Penelope to Ulysses in which Colonna refers to the imprisonment of her father and her husband after the battle of Ravenna in 1512.[62] But the performance of a letter as a musical piece, whether it is by a female or male musician, nevertheless exerts a kind of emotional control over the words, deceptive or not.

---

[58] Rosenmeyer, *Ancient Epistolary Fictions*, 209–12, pp. 307–309; one may think here again of Captain Wentworth's letter to Anne Elliot in Jane Austen's novel *Persuasion* (1817) which contains the arresting line: 'You pierce my soul'.
[59] Farrell, 'Reading and Writing the *Heroides*', p. 322.
[60] See Spentzou, 'Postcards Home', pp. 123–60.
[61] Farrell, 'Reading and Writing the *Heroides*', p. 322.
[62] See Cox, *Lyric Poetry by Women of the Italian Renaissance*, pp. 77–82.

2 The Epistolary Madrigal

> *Just as we used to spend long hours in talk*
> *until the day ended with us still talking,*
> *so now our letters should carry forth and bring back our silent voices,*
> *and paper and hands perform the tasks of our tongues.*[63]
> —Ovid

The early history of sung love letters reaches back at least to the Renaissance. Alfred Einstein was one of the few, and probably the first, to write about the *lettera amorosa* as a musical genre.[64] His discussion, like most on the subject, was anchored around Claudio Monteverdi's famous *lettera amorosa* – a setting of Claudio Achillini's text 'Se i languidi miei sguardi' – first published in the Seventh Book of madrigals of 1619. Einstein's interest stemmed from a desire to codify the defining stylistic characteristics of the letter in the declamatory recitation of the *genere rappresentativo*. He identified the very first *lettera amorosa* as a *frottola*, 'Adspicias utinam', written before 1516 by the composer Bartolomeo Tromboncino ($c.$1470–$c.$1535).[65] The piece, which first appeared in print in Andrea Antico's *Il secondo libro di frottole*, is a Latin setting of Dido's letter from Ovid's *Heroides* VII.[66] It is exceptionally long for a *frottola*. The text comprises the final fourteen lines of Dido's letter; the music is through-composed, and affords an affecting and emotionally potent variety in figuration.[67] Its dating suggests that it was likely composed while Tromboncino was in the service of Lucrezia Borgia – the illegitimate daughter of Cardinal Rodrigo de Borgia (later Pope Alexander VI) — and Cardinal Ippolito d'Este – brother both to Lucrezia's husband Duke Alfonso I d'Este Duke of Ferrara and to her sister-in-law Isabella d'Este.[68]

Much like the other letters from Ovid's *Heroides*, Tromboncino's excerpted text invites listeners to see the image of the benighted writer by listening to her words. The piece begins: 'Adspicias utinam, quae sit scribentis imago!' ('Could you but see now the face of her who writes these words!'). As she writes Dido's tears roll down her cheeks to stain not the paper, but the reflective steel of a blade, soon to be covered in blood, 'qui iam pro lacrimis sanguine tinctus erit' (full text in online Appendix 2.1,

---

[63] Ovid, *Tristia* 5.13, 27–30; trans. Rosenmeyer, *Ancient Epistolary Fictions*, p. 98.
[64] Einstein, 'La prima "lettera amorosa" in musica', pp. 45–52.
[65] Prizer notes that the piece was composed even earlier than Einstein's dating of 1516 owing to the fact that editions of Antico's second book of *frottole* were published in 1512 or 1513 as well as in 1516. See Prizer, *Courtly Pastimes*, p. 327.
[66] To my knowledge there are no other settings of Ovid's original text from the *Heroides* in this period. One exception is the piece 'Constant Penelope' by William Byrd, which sets a portion of an English translation of Ovid's letter for Penelope (no. 23 in his *Psalmes, Sonnets, and Songs* of 1588).
[67] See Prizer, *Courtly Pastimes*, p. 106.
[68] Prizer, 'Isabella d'Este and Lucrezia Borgia as Patrons of Music', 1–33 (p. 22).

available at www.cambridge.org/lettera-amorosa).[69] The shared vocality between letters and epitaphs seen in Section 1 is brought to bear at the end of Tromboncino's piece in which the singer, who may up until this point have been equated with Dido herself, sings aloud the words to be inscribed into the marble of the queen's tomb: 'let this brief epitaph be read on the marble of my tomb: From Aeneas came the cause of her death, and from him the blade; from the hand of Dido herself came the stroke by which she fell'.[70] At this point the 'reader' adopts the voice of another, switching from mimesis to diegesis, and instead 'reads' as might anyone who sees and hears Dido's plight. Tromboncino breaks the contrapuntal flow with moments of homophony to mark the juncture in which the poetic voice shifts (Example 1).[71]

Einstein provides a transcription of Tromboncino's *lettera* in which only the highest singing voice is given the text and the lower four voices are reduced to two staves. While this may indeed reflect common performance practice for early sixteenth-century *frottole* – that is, with the top voice sung and the rest played instrumentally – the lower voices nevertheless show contrapuntal complexity, as Francesco Luisi's edition underscores.[72] Einstein's transcription seeks to provide a lineage for Monteverdi's *lettera amorosa*, writing that Tromboncino's setting of Ovid is 'a monody one century before the advent of monody'.[73] One may point out, however, that Tromboncino's *frottola* need not be a 'monody in disguise' to be a precursor to the *lettere amorose* of the early Seicento. In the case of the musical love letter, as indeed with monody itself, generic or chronological continuity is not the necessary factor in determining its resilience as a mode of expression.

There are few examples of musical settings of epistolary poetry between Tromboncino's *frottola* in the early decades of the sixteenth century and the madrigals in the early decades of the seventeenth century. This does not reflect the proliferation of fictional letters published in this period, particularly by women writers such as Vittoria Colonna, Isabella Andreini, and Margherita Costa. There is a similar gap in the chronology between the madrigals and monodies of the early Seicento and the cantatas in the latter part of the century. The earlier secular musical genres of the Renaissance including much of the *frottola* tradition relied only

---

[69] See full text in Online Appendix 2.1. Note the use of the authorial plural 'scribimus' which was also used by Briseis in *Heroides* III (see Section 1). See also Spentzou, *Readers and Writers in Ovid's Heroides*, p. 111.

[70] 'Hoc tantum in tumuli marmore carmen erit: | Praebuit Aeneas et causam mortis et ensem; | ipsa sua Dido concidit usa manu'.

[71] The text underlay in Example 1 follows the edition by Luisi, *Il secondo libro di frottola di Andrea Antico*, ii, pp. 139–50.

[72] Luisi, *Il secondo libro di frottola di Andrea Antico*, i, pp. 330–32; ii, pp. 139–50.

[73] Einstein, 'La prima "lettera amorosa" in musica', p. 47. For a more recent engagement of Ovid in music and of opera in particular see Heller, 'Ovid's Ironic Gaze', 203–225; Heller, 'Hypsipyle, Medea, and the Ovidian Imagination', 167–86; and her forthcoming monograph *Animating Ovid: Opera and the Metamorphosis of Antiquity in Early Modern Italy*.

Example 1 Bartolomeo Tromboncino, 'Adspicias utinam', mm. 107–20.

partially or not at all on musical notation. As we will see, epistolary texts may have been sung during the fifteenth and sixteenth centuries through practices in which musical composition is indistinguishable from performance. But the *lettera amorosa* is inherently tied with explicitly written representation, and this may explain its delineation in the early decades of the seventeenth century. Still, the *lettera amorosa* seems not to have been bound by a particular musical genre or style; it has been, at various historical moments, a *frottola*, a madrigal, a monody in *genere rappresentativo*, and a cantata. What links these pieces together is their 'epistolary intent' and the erotic paradox of voice in its sensory manifestations.

The lack of musical love letters between the early and late decades of the sixteenth century may be somewhat illusory. Both the nature and the prevalence of epistolary poetry from Italian courtly circles suggest a hidden musical history. While Tromboncino's *frottola* is significant for being an early setting with a text directly from Ovid's *Heroides*, it is certainly not the earliest *lettera amorosa*, notated or not.

In his study of performance practice of the *frottola* repertory, H. Colin Slim briefly mentions the text of a popular *epistola* written in *terza rima*, 'Non expectò già mai con tal desio', by the Ferrarese poet Antonio Tebaldeo (1463–1537).[74] The text seems to have been very well known and widely disseminated (online Appendix 2.2). Not only does it appear in numerous manuscripts, prints, and pamphlets from around the early to mid sixteenth century, it was also certainly set to music by 1502.[75] It appears as a three-voice *frottola* by an anonymous composer in *F-Pn*, ms Rés. Vm^7 676, a manuscript copied in Mantua for the court of Isabella d'Este (Figure 5).[76] Several other musical settings must have appeared in the years

Figure 5 Anonymous, 'Non expecto giamai cum tal disio' (1502), *F-Pn*, ms. Rés. Vm^7 676, 27^v–28

---

[74] Slim, 'Valid and Invalid Options for Performing Frottole', pp. 323–26. The tradition of writing poetic letters in *terza rima* endured into the seventeenth century. In tracing the literary history of the poetic letter Robert Holzer points to Francesco della Valle's collection of fourteen letters, also in *terza rima*, entitled *Le lettere delle dame, e degli eroi* (Venice: Ciotti, 1622) and Bruni's *Epistole eroiche*. The latter began to abandon *terza rima* in favour of *versi sciolti*. See Holzer, 'Music and Poetry in Seventeenth-Century Rome: Settings of the Canzonetta and Cantata Texts', p. 268.

[75] See Tebaldeo, *Rime*, ii, 1, pp. 425–39. The 1502 anonymous setting includes the first eight stanzas of Tebaldeo's text.

[76] The copyist's name appears several times in the manuscript and is given as Lodovicus Millias or Millaire. The manuscript is dated 1502. See Bridgman, 'Un manuscrit italien du début du XVIe siècle', 177–267 (p. 206); Prizer, 'Paris, Bibliothéque Nationale MS Rés. Vm^7 676 and Music at Mantua', pp. 235–39. A facsimile edition can be found in Lesure, *Manuscrit italien de frottola (1502)*, p. 7 and pp. 46–47.

which followed;[77] the first with a known composer is one by Ansano Senese (*c*.1470– *c*.1524) whose two-stanza setting of Tebaldeo's *epistola* appeared in Pietro Sambonetto's *Canzoni sonetti strambotti et frottole libro primo* published in Siena in 1515.[78]

Tebaldeo's *capitolo* was widely distributed in print sources and is singled out in several printed pamphlets, some of which appear with images and accompanying texts. While none of these appears to contain music, there are other sources which suggest that the musical life of this epistolary poem was by no means limited to notated musical settings. The simplicity and structural regularity of even the Mantuan *frottola* suggest that Tebaldeo's letter was conducive to oral composition: it may have often been sung with the aid of musical formulae and complemented in practice by improvisations. The appearance of Tebaldeo's letter in a 1515 engraving by Agostino de' Musi (*c*.1490– *c*.1540), *detto* Agostino Veneziano, further suggests that it was strongly associated with musical performance. The print, modelled on a design by Baccio Bandinelli (*c*.1493–*c*.1560), depicts a robust male nude seated on a rock at the base of a tree in the foreground of a town landscape (Figure 6). At the figure's right hand is an open partbook with two staves of music fitted with the 'crudely lettered' opening line of Tebaldeo's *epistola*: 'Non aspeto giamai con tal [desio]'.[79]

Tebaldeo's letter is written from a woman's perspective; she excoriates her absent lover for failing to return, quoting back to him his own letter which falsely claims that his arrival would be imminent. The artifice of the poetic exercise is acknowledged in a brief preface that accompanies early prints of Tebaldeo's text: '*Epistola* by Tebaldeo of Ferrara who imagines that a lady wrote it and sent it to him'.[80] The letter may be 'feigned', but its musical life certainly was not. If 'Non expectò già mai cum tal desio' is sung in humanistic fashion by the male poet, the performance creates an unusual situation in which a male voice is commandeered by the words of a woman. This is in contrast to what occurs in the writing of the poem in which the male voice 'creates' the female perspective. The lady's words recount the anxiety of her expectancy asking, somewhat ironically, 'Who forced you then, when you wrote to me: "Endure it! Expect! Expect that I will come without delay"?' ('Ahimè, crudel, chi te sforzava alhora, | quando scrivesti a me: 'Soporta, expetta! | Expetta, ch'io verrò senza dimora!').

---

[77] A four-voice version from *c*.1505 setting only the first stanza survives in a source from northern Italy (*I-Fn*, ms Panciatichi 27, 17ʳ, 4ᵛ).

[78] This may be the only book of printed music to survive from sixteenth-century Siena. See Jeppesen, *La Frottola*, i, pp. 59–62 and D'Accone, 'Instrumental Resonances in a Sienese Vocal Print of 1515', p. 333 and 336, 17n.

[79] Slim, 'Valid and Invalid Options for Performing Frottole', p. 323.

[80] 'Epistola del Tibaldeo de Ferrara che finge chel habia facta una donna e mandata a lui', in *Epistola del Tibaldeo* (*c*. 1495), Biblioteca Casanatense, Rome, Vol. Inc. 1729; 'Sa' in Tebaldeo, *Rime*, i, p. 109.

Figure 6 Agostino Veneziano (after Baccio Bandinelli), 'Male Nude with Music Book' (1515), The British Museum

Her quotation of his untruthful and misleading words would be a kind of retaliation in performance, as his receiving voice is the one forced to utter them.

One print of Tebaldeo's letter from about 1515 is accompanied by an image of the epistolary exchange implied in the poem. It depicts a woman giving a man a letter with her left hand and gesturing to him with her right while Cupid above aims his arrow at her.[81] The implication is that while she has been struck by love, her love is not or cannot be returned, for, while accepting her letter, he is not likewise struck by love's arrow. Indeed, the print reproduced in Figure 7, as with several others of this text from about the same time, includes an apologetic

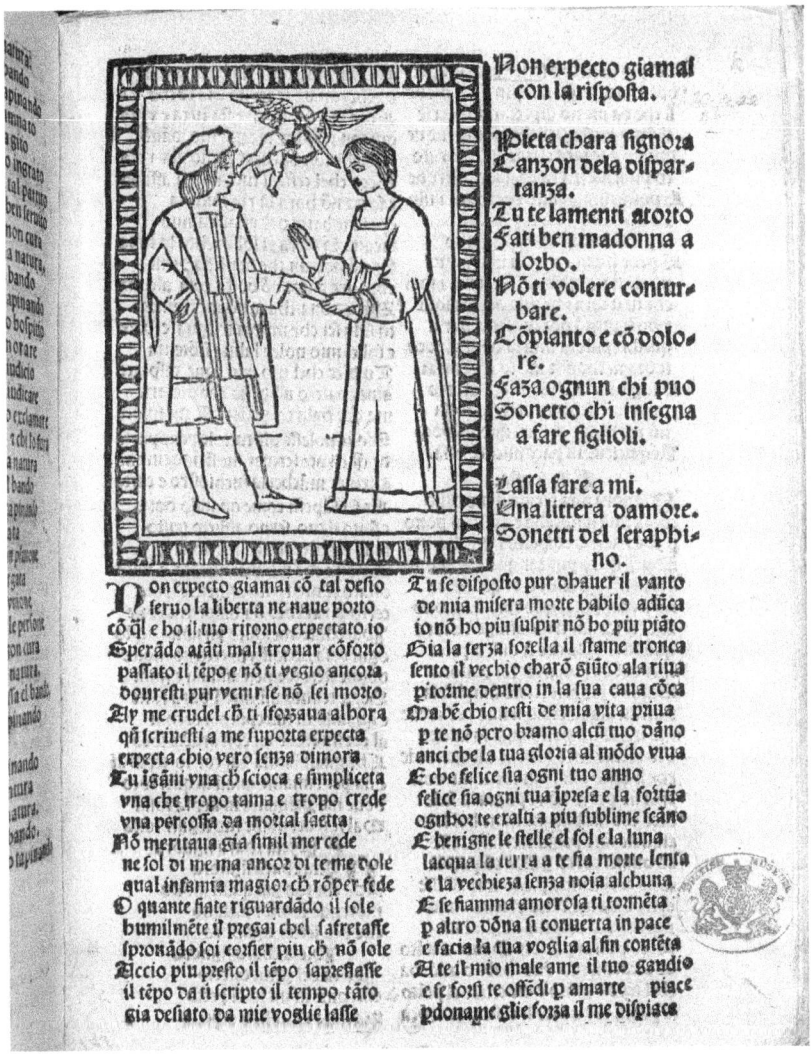

Figure 7 Antonio Tebaldeo, 'Non expecto giamai. Con la Risposta' (*c.* 1515?), British Library (C.20 c.22 [26]).

---

[81] It is worth noting that the gesture and the exchange are ambiguous, even in the image; in another print of Tebaldeo's text (Biblioteca Riccardiana, Florence, early sixteenth century) it is the man who is struck by Cupid's arrow, not the woman.

'risposta' from the absent man to his lady. The 'response' comes in the form of a verse epistle 'Signora mia, ferma il tuo disio' on the page following and, in other print versions, the text ends with a prose letter as well subtitled 'littera overo epistola da mandare a una innamorata'.[82]

That the poems by Tebaldeo were strongly associated with musical performance is further corroborated by the presence in these prints of several poems by Serafino Aquilano (1466–1500), the Neapolitan musician known throughout Italy for his improvisations of music and poetry. Among other poems, an early print of 'Non expectò già mai cum tal desio' from about 1495 currently in the Biblioteca Casanatense in Rome includes the text of Serafino's *barzelletta* 'Vox clamantis in deserto'. This poem too had a colourful musical life: Ottaviano Petrucci included a setting of the poem in his *Frottole libro tertio* (Venice, 150[5]) and attributed it to none other than Bartolomeo Tromboncino. While Petrucci's authorial designation cannot be confirmed with certainty, Tromboncino may well have set 'Vox clamantis in deserto' to music when one considers the tastes both musical and poetic of his patron in Mantua: Isabella d'Este. But the issue of authorship may be beside the point since it seems equally likely that some of the music in Petrucci's print could instead be transcriptions of Serafino's performances.[83]

In conjunction with the improvisatory traces in the poem itself, the musical life of the poem therefore reflects a history of oral composition. Tebaldeo's 'Non expectò già mai cum tal desio' is different in this respect; its content is self-consciously written and any performance of it would explicitly reveal its epistolary intent. The early written musical settings of Tebaldeo's text link it more closely with the *lettere amorose* of the decades following than with the unwritten secular traditions of the early Renaissance despite their notable cultural affinities. The improvisatory nature of the *lettera amorosa* in the early sixteenth century was transformed in the seventeenth century to a much more circumscribed 'written' practice of composing musical love letters not as *frottole* but as madrigals and monodies.

The first three decades of the seventeenth century saw the greatest number of musical settings of epistolary poetry. The monodic *lettere amorose* of Monteverdi, Sigismondo d'India, Girolamo Frescobaldi and several others tended to set substantially long texts in free-rhyming *versi sciolti*. Also in vogue were settings of much more concise epistolary texts: madrigals, sonnets,

---

[82] The prose letter begins 'Perche son stato alli di passata molto ad voi unica mia Madonna' in a print from the early sixteenth century (*Capitolo de non espetto giamai. Con la risposta. Et altra canzone*) currently in the Biblioteca Riccardiana in Florence.

[83] MacNeil, 'A Voice Crying in the Wilderness', pp. 463–76. See also Wilson, *Singing the Lyre in Renaissance Italy*.

and *canzone* by the leading Italian poets of the day. There was great diversity, in other words, both in the type of poetry which could be cast as a *lettera amorosa*, but also in musical textures and styles. While the recitative-style pieces in and around the time of Monteverdi's *lettera* are the most extensive examples of musical letters, others were polyphonic madrigals, *canzonette*, *concertato* pieces with *basso continuo* for two, three, or more voices. They all appeared, with few exceptions, in printed madrigal books from the turn of the seventeenth century through to about 1640, and directly reflected the increasing stylistic heterogeneity those collections afforded. What links this diverse pool of musical pieces is not just the peculiar vocality of 'epistolary intent' traced so far, but also the stylistic *concettismo* of the late sixteenth and early seventeenth century. The erotic paradoxes of the verse letter found new life in the epistolary poems of Claudio Achillini (1574–1640), Girolamo Preti (1582–1626), and above all Giambattista Marino (1569–1625), who gave his name to the bejewelled poetics of Marinism.

There is a rich assortment of poems from the turn of the seventeenth century that could be interpreted as *lettere amorose* (online Appendix 1); their variety, in both style and structure, had consequences for the way they were set to music. The mere mention of writing and its implements could certainly evoke the physicality and tactility of letters, but it did not necessarily mean that the poem itself was to stand in as a letter, in the manner of a transcript. In many poems, madrigals and sonnets mainly, the poetry is addressed not to an actual recipient, but to the letter itself. In these cases, the epistolary of the poem is truly a stylistic conceit; the poet 'talks' to the letter he or she is writing, willing it to act as a messenger who will transport their heart and soul to the beloved. Despite not being actual letters, strictly speaking, such poems were still considered *lettere amorose*. While the designation may have been applied quite liberally in the early decades of the seventeenth century, such pieces still engaged the kind of perspectival ambiguity so central to the *lettera amorosa*. If the addressee is the letter itself, or perhaps if the writer 'speaks' through the letter itself, the identities of 'I', 'you', 'she' and 'he' are still complicated by the practicalities of musical performance. Who is speaking and to whom or through whom are they communicating? And the act of concealing the contents of a letter can be just as intriguing and, indeed, erotic as the act of revealing them. In this way, the performance of such musical love letters can provide a real-time analogue for the experience of viewing the letter paintings of the Dutch artists of the seventeenth century (see Prologue): 'What is suggested in the pictures is not the content of the letters, the lovers' feelings, their plans to meet, or the practice and the experience of love, but rather the letter as an object of visual attention, a surface to be looked at'.[84]

---

[84] Alpers, *The Art of Describing*, p. 196.

Marino called his 'Foglio de' miei pensieri', a madrigal published in the second part of his *Rime* (1602), a 'lettera amorosa'. The poem is part of a sequence of *lettere amorose* including three other texts frequently set to music: 'Vanne, carta felice', 'Queste dogliose stille', and 'In queste bianche carte'.[85] 'Foglio, de' miei pensieri' is a meditation on the love letter as the faithful secretary who dispatches the writer's heart. The poet imagines the beautiful hands of the beloved unfolding the letter and, in the same manner, opening the envelope to his heart: 'folio of my thoughts, faithful secretary, you will go where that hand which opens you, opens my breast' ('foglio, de' miei pensieri | secretario fedel, tu n'andrai dove | t'aprirà quella man, che m'apre il petto'). The poem was set to music for two voices by Enrico Radesca da Foggia, organist and *maestro di cappella* at the Savoy court in Turin, and appeared in his fourth book of *canzonette* of 1610 in which the piece is also labelled 'lettera amorosa'. Sigismondo d'India, who, like both Marino and Radesca had ties to the court in Turin, also set the poem to music in his Second Book of five-voice madrigals in 1611.

The musicality of poetic letters in which the epistolary is treated as a poetic conceit was sometimes quite literal. Marino's intriguing text 'Le note, ove son chiusi i miei tormenti' ('The notes, where my torments are enclosed') tells of a female singer, a 'cantatrice', who reads or rather sings the poet's lamenting words which, as sweet accents from so sweet a mouth, become pleasing to him. The text itself is not a letter, but the performative situation it describes, in which a singer 'reads' ('legge') through song ('canti il mio canto'), is analogous to the musical delivery of a *lettera amorosa* (see text and translation in online Appendix 2.3).

The musical nature of 'Le note, ove son chiusi i miei tormenti', unsurprisingly, afforded it at least five musical settings including two for solo voice by Bartolomeo Barberino, *detto* il Pesarino (*III a1*, 1610) and Vincenzo Calestani (*Madrigali e arie a1–2*, 1617), two for five voices by Alessandro Scialla (*I a5*, 1610) and Vincenzo Dal Pozzo *(IV a5*, 1612), and one as a cantata for two voices by Carlo Caprioli (*detto* Carluccio del Violino) preserved in a late seventeenth-century manuscript (I-Bc, Q.48). The poem's grammatical peculiarities create rather different performative scenarios in these various voice configurations: each composer may have read the poem rather differently. As a solo piece the lady, possibly equated with the singer, is enacting what the text says she is doing. But there is a problem. She, as the 'cantatrice de' versi dell'auttore', may in fact be reading as she sings, but she is speaking not in her own voice but as someone else talking about her. The address is in the third person ('legge Maddona', 'my lady [she] reads') and, consequently, at a remove from the performer. The lady can hardly tell herself to sing while singing: 'ami, e canti il mio canto' ('you love, and sing my song'): and

---

[85] Marino, *La lira 1614*, pp. 314–15.

yet she does. Even though the text is quite clear in that it is the poet and writer who is speaking to or as the letter (the woman's voice does not sound here), a musical performance of this piece could scarcely suggest that the singing being described is not connected with the singing currently being heard. If we take the text at face value the situation would be an odd one: the poet is telling the audience (through song) about the letter that he may or may not have written to another woman who presumably reads the letter in another, imagined, musical performance. Calestani's solo voice setting from 1617 does little to clarify the situation since in his setting the music is notated with a C1 clef and suggests a performance by a soprano (Example 2). A fundamental ambiguity remains, even in the rather different situation in which the setting includes two or more singers. In Scialla's setting for five voices, one may now imagine several voices standing in for the poet or writer but the question of when, where, and by whom the 'music' of this poem occurs and, intriguingly, what kind of sound it makes is unclear (Example 3).

An analogous situation exists with a very similar text, 'O carta avventurosa', which is a variation on Marino's aforementioned 'Foglio, de' miei pensieri'. In this case, the letter is sent forth as a 'messaggiera d'amore' ('messenger of love') and 'secretaria del core' ('secretary of the heart'). Like 'Le note, ove son chiusi i miei tormenti', 'O carta avventurosa' was also set both for solo voice by Claudio Saracini in his *Terze musiche* (1620), and for five voices, by Amadio Freddi in his Second Book (1614). Even if the perspectival orientation of these poems is, at least grammatically, unambiguous – they are virtuoso meditations about letters – the situations they describe betray a complex relationship between words read and words heard. Composers seem to have read the embedded performativity of the texts – written speech that gets respoken in song – through a variety of different vocal and stylistic configurations.

The vast majority of *lettere amorose* that appear to be literal transcripts of letters are longer texts in *versi sciolti* or rhymed couplets, whereas the poems that treat letters as poetic conceits tend to be shorter madrigals and sonnets. The categories, however, are not mutually exclusive, neither poetically nor musically. Musical styles and textures do not, therefore, line up neatly with the form or perspectival orientation of the text: solo voice settings are not reserved exclusively for actual letters in *versi sciolti* any more than madrigals and sonnets that treat letters as poetic conceits are always multi-voice settings. For example, the second of Marino's *lettere amorose* in the sequence from *La Lira II* is 'Vanne, carta felice' ('Go, happy paper') (online Appendix 2.4). The poem, like Marino's other madrigal love letters, is specifically labelled 'lettera amorosa' and shifts in line four from addressing the letter itself to giving quoted 'speech' that the letter is meant to communicate to the beloved upon reaching its destination. While in Marino's poem it is the letter herself that 'speaks', it is unclear if this is a fantasy of the writer

Example 2 Vincenzo Calestani, 'Le note, ove son chiusi i miei tormenti', mm. 1–7

Example 3 Alessandro Scialla, 'Le note, ove son chiusi i miei tormenti', mm. 20–7

Example 3 (Cont.)

who imagines the letter flying to the beloved and telling her what he does not or cannot say, or if these recited words are in fact the contents of the letter itself: for letters can only speak by the words they contain. Both the letter and the lady are addressed with the informal 'tu' implying that the quoted speech, as the words of the inanimate letter 'speaking' to the beloved, are really the refracted words of the writer which only reach their destination mediated as a letter.[86]

Marino's madrigal 'Queste dogliose stille' is a particularly interesting case, both in the diversity of musical responses it inspired, and its poignant

---

[86] The poem was set to music in Basilio Cossa's *Madrigaletti a tre voci* (Venice, 1617). The 'I' in the quoted speech is feminine ('secura') and represents the letter herself ('la lettera').

distillation of the classical tradition. The poem, which Marino prefaces with the phrase 'Rime mandate alla sua Donna', opens with the Ovidian conflation of ink drops with teardrops. Upon first glance, the poem appears, like many of the madrigal texts seen so far, to be a meditation upon a piece of writing instead of the actual text of a letter. Everything changes when the poet addresses his 'Donna celeste' directly by writing 'a te le 'nvio'('to you I send them'), implying that the sorrowful drops ('dogliose stille') are in fact the messengers of love ('messaggiere d'Amore') and that this poem is itself what he sends to her. The use of the informal address in the form of the second person singular ('a te') is, much like the imperative command ('read!'), yet another distinctive characteristic seen in many *lettere amorose* texts.[87] It is also one of the ways in which love letters share a similar psychology to laments, a point to which we will return.

Queste dogliose stille,	These sorrowful drops,
inchiostri no, ma pianti,	not of ink, but of weeping,
pianti no, ma faville,	not weeping, but sparks,
di nere note, e meste	of sorrowful black notes
fabricate, e conteste,[88]	composed and interwoven,
specchi loquaci ai lagrimosi amanti,	loquacious mirrors to tear-filled lovers,
non sdegnar, non sprezzar Donna celeste,	do not scorn, do not disdain, celestial Lady,
a te le 'nvio: son queste messaggiere d'Amore,	to you I send them: these are messengers of Love,
son figlie di quest'occhi, anzi del core.[89]	they are the children of these eyes, or rather of this heart.

In 'Queste dogliose stille' Marino crafts a syntactic chain of metaphors through which the writer doubts, rethinks, and revises what the ink drops are and what they represent. The brief rhetorical anadiplosis of the opening lines gives way to the letters as 'black notes' – 'di nere note' – the written signs that both reflect and compete with their metaphorical referents. The notes are

---

[87] The use of the informal address in Torquato Tasso's poem 'Se tu mi lasci, perfida/perfido, tuo danno', set as a five-voice madrigal in Monteverdi's Second Book (1590), may explain why it has been interpreted as a letter poem by at least one editor of Tasso's verses. In an edition of Tasso's *Rime* from 1608 published in Venice by Evangelista Deuchino and Giovanni Battista Pulciani, the poem is given a preface that reads it as a letter from a rejected lover: 'Tutto adirato scrive alla poco amica sua, non [illegible] d'esser da lei per altri abbandonato'. See the literary variants for this poem in the Tasso in Music Project.

[88] 'Fabricate e conteste' refer both to the composition of the 'dogliose stille' – the fact that they are 'made' – but also to the literal fabric and weaving (*tessuto*) of the words (*textus*) onto the paper. I am grateful to Eugenio Refini for pointing this out.

[89] Marino, *La lira (1614)*, II, mad. 107, p. 315.

composed in weeping ('pianti') but are at the same time sparks or embers ('faville'); they weave the two together into a fabric that makes manifest an emotionally real but physically impossible coexistence. The drops of tears staining the paper cannot extinguish the passionate flames communicated therein any more than the words can burn the wetness of the tears: they are literally woven together in a tightly knit fabric. This makes an interesting counterpoint with 'Vanne, carta felice' – one of the two other poems Marino casts as *lettere amorose* – in which the 'wetness' of the tear-soaked letter instead provides the 'notes' protection from the fiery gaze of the beloved that would otherwise burn the paper. Such a notational play on words was by no means lost on the composers who set these verses to music. In some madrigal settings, the moment is marked with a pun simultaneously visual and aural. In the earliest setting of the poem for five voices by Giovanni Bernardo Colombi (*I a5*, 1603; Figure 8), and in a later one for solo voice by Marc Antonio Negri (*Affetti amorosi*, 1611), the line 'di nere note' uses coloration to indicate a temporary switch from duple to triple time.[90]

Marino's text evokes images and themes central to the tradition of verse letters in antiquity. The letters formed by the inkblots are further characterized as 'loquacious mirrors', the reflective surface upon which the reader may 'see' the image of their lover as well as themselves. In Adriano Banchieri's five-voice setting of 'Queste dogliose stille', published in his *Vivezze di Flora e primavera* (1622), the line 'specchi loquaci ai lagrimosi amanti' is set to a distinctive spiral-like circular figure that cycles self-reflexively through the polyphonic texture.[91] Similarly, Giovanni Ceresini draws particular attention to the line in his *concertato* setting for two tenors from 1627 by fitting it with an extended passage in dotted rhythms and repeating it four times (Example 4).[92] The concise *concettismo* of letters as poetic madrigals therefore inspired an appropriately concerted approach in their musical setting. The images evoked in these texts nevertheless reach back to the epistolary fictions of antiquity and, in the longer epistolary poems of the seventeenth century, create even more overt play on voice and perspective.

The *lettera amorosa* is not merely an interaction between reader and writer. The epistolary poems of the early seventeenth century reveal that the communicative complexity of the mode is not restricted to this dichotomy. The voice of the writer

---

[90] There is also a brief passage in triple time at the line 'fabricate e conteste' in a three-voice *concertato* setting Marino's madrigal by Bonifacio Graziani (who was at the time *maestro di cappella* in Rome at the church of the Gesù and the Seminario Romano) from the 1653 miscellany *Florido concento di madrigali in musica ... parte seconda* (Rome: Vitale Mascardi, 1653).
[91] Banchieri, *Vivezze di flora e primavera* (1622), pp. 80–84, mm. 11–12.
[92] Ceresini, *Madrigali concertati a due tre e quattro voci*.

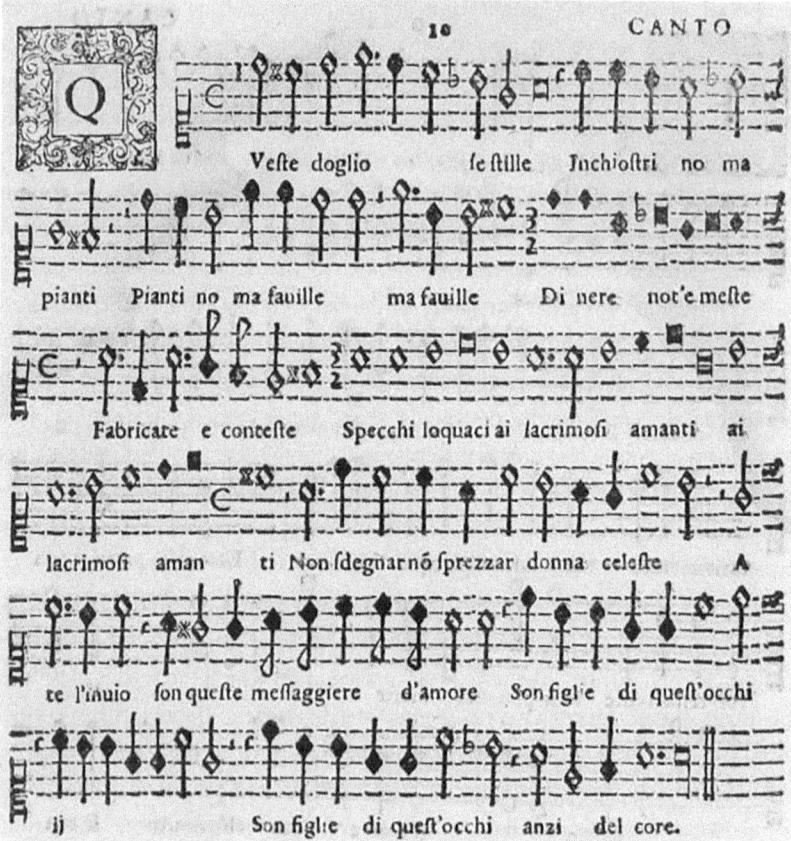

Figure 8 Giovanni Bernardo Colombi, *Primo libro de madrigali* (Venice, 1603), p. 10, Biblioteca Estense Universitaria

may speak through the letter voiced by the recipient but also to it, further complicating the identity of the singer or singers who perform it. Marinist poet Girolamo Preti's 'Vanne, o carta amorosa', set in part to music by Girolamo Frescobaldi (*Secondo libro d'arie musicali*, 1630), is a lengthy idyll in *versi sciolti* in which the addressee throughout the poem is the letter self-reflexively, not the beloved.[93] This *lettera amorosa* will be discussed in greater detail in Section 4, but it is worth pointing out that in Preti's text, the lover is not really speaking to his beloved – he writes not to her directly, but in fact addresses the physical letter. The representation actually represents itself. 'Go, o love letter', the text reads, 'go to her for whom I die

---

[93] 'Vanne, o carta amorosa' is the first piece in Frescobaldi's *Secondo libro d'arie musicali* (Florence: Landini, 1630). Preti's text was also set to music for two voices by Giovanni Valentini in his *Musiche a2* (1622); see Whenham, *Duet and Dialogue in the Age of Monteverdi*, ii, pp. 251–55.

Example 4 Giovanni Ceresini, 'Queste dogliose stille', mm. 13–21

in silence: ... O my timid letter, you burn, and hope and pray. Ask her, ask her for pity towards my love and my faith but no recompense'.

The fact that this *lettera amorosa* does not reveal its contents but creates the situation in which the listener may indirectly infer the circumstances of the lovers' desire is analogous to the melancholy play of letters in seventeenth-century painting seen in the Prologue. Like Frescobaldi's setting of Preti, Biagio Marini's 1618 setting of Marino's sonnet 'Le carte, in ch'io primier scrissi e mostrai' too is written for solo voice in recitative even though the text playfully withholds the contents of the letter instead of giving it. The poem set by Marini is a play on the idea of 'printing' love bites according to a manual on the art of kissing that the beloved Lillia is requesting from her lover.[94] In making the play on reciprocity audible though, the love letter oscillates between the tangible and intangible marks of amorous desire. As John Donne writes in his verse letter to the diplomat Sir Henry Wotton, 'more than kisses, letters mingle souls'.[95]

---

[94] Marini, *Madrigali et Symfonie (1618)*, pp. 111–12 The text appears in the third part of Marino's *La lira*, 'Amori': Marino, *La lira (1614)*, p. 454.

[95] Donne, *The Complete English Poems*, p. 214.

3 Monteverdi's Love Letters

> *Non è gia parte in voi*
> *che, con forza invisible d'amore,*
> *tutto a sé non mi tragga.*
>
> *There is no part of you*
> *which, with the invisible power of love,*
> *does not draw me into itself.*

This arresting passage comes from what is arguably the most influential musical love letter of the early seventeenth century: Claudio Monteverdi's 'Se i languidi miei sguardi', an extensive piece for solo voice in *genere rappresentativo* first published in *Concerto. Settimo libro de madrigali* of 1619. The poet of the *lettera* was long unknown, but this same passage was used centuries after Monteverdi's death to preface another, very different, poetic love letter. The French poet René Char (1907–88) took inspiration from Monteverdi (the poet Claudio Achillini's name is not mentioned) in his own *lettera amorosa* of 1953, which he revised to appear at the head of his collection *La parole en archipel* in 1962. Char's poem is, like its unacknowledged predecessor, a meditation on desire distilled into an epistle. He writes of the psychology of the love letter as if it were the manifestation of a dormant, invisible, and yet ubiquitous gravitational force which allows voices separated in time and space to flow freely one from the other.

> Nos paroles sont lentes à nous parvenir, comme si elles contenaient, séparées, une sève suffisante pour rester closes tout un hiver; ou mieux, comme si, à chaque extrémité de la silencieuse distance, se mettant en joue, il leur était interdit de s'élancer et de se joindre. Notre voix court de l'un à l'autre.
>
> Our words are slow to come to us, as though they contained, separated, enough sap to remain closed all one winter; or better, as if at each end of the silent distance, taking aim at one another, they were not permitted to spring forth and join. Our voices flow between us.[96]

Some years later, the Italian writer Riccardo Bacchelli (1891–1985) wrote a poem in hendecasyllables dedicated to the 'two Claudios': his Bolognese compatriot Claudio Achillini and, of course, Claudio Monteverdi. In his 'Sulla "Lettera amorosa" di Achillini e Monteverdi' the poet writes of the celestial music to which the *lettera amorosa* was set, and to the parallel, cosmic force that led the Bacchelli himself to divine the name of hitherto unknown poet. Although it was Claudio Gallico who, in an article from 1967, recognized Achillini as the poet of Monteverdi's *lettera amorosa*, he writes in a footnote that it was in fact Bacchelli

---

[96] Char, *La parole en archipel*, p. 18.

who initially made the connection, as the last stanza of the poem implies (text and translation in online Appendix 3.1).[97] The interest that both Char and Bacchelli had in seventeenth-century poetry and music may at first be surprising, but the erotic paradoxes they found there resonate anew in the reciprocal vocality of their own amorous discourse. It is perhaps fitting in this light to consider that Luciano Berio's (1925–2003) *Recital I (for Cathy)*, first performed in 1972, begins by quoting the music of Monteverdi's *lettera amorosa*.[98]

The text of Monteverdi's *lettera amorosa* is undoubtedly Marinist in persuasion and was, on at least one occasion, mistakenly attributed to Marino himself.[99] The poem is, as Gallico has shown, a heavily redacted version of a lengthy epistolary idyll by Claudio Achillini. It survives in several different versions following its first appearance in the 1612 collection *L'amorosa ambasciatrice*, published in Vicenza by Francesco Grossi, in which the author is given simply as A.C.[100] Achillini was a close friend to Marino. He was one of the poets, along with one of Monteverdi's librettists Giacomo Badoaro, whose tribute letters were published in the first posthumous edition of Marino's letters in 1627. Monteverdi would turn to Achillini's verses on three other occasions. A setting of the poet's sonnet 'Ecco vicine, o bella tigre, l'ore' appeared in the Seventh Book alongside the two *lettere amorose*. Some years later, Monteverdi set two pieces of Achillini's theatrical texts performed during the Medici-Farnese wedding festivities at Parma in December of 1628: the prologue *Teti e Flora* for a performance of Tasso's play *Aminta* with *intermedi* by Ascanio Pio di Savoia, and the tournament *Mercurio e Marte* for the newly inaugurated Teatro Farnese.

How Monteverdi acquired the text for Achillini's *lettera amorosa* and when, precisely, he wrote the piece is not certain. Some have speculated that a lengthy monody would have been anachronistic by 1619, the year the Seventh Book was published, raising the possibility that it was composed some years earlier.[101] The supposed stylistic anachronism does not, on the other hand, explain why the 'Se i languidi miei sguardi' was included in an even later print from 1623 in which it is paired with another 'letter' *in genere rappresentativo* – Ottavio Rinuccini's 'Se pur destina e vòle' called a *partenza amorosa* in Monteverdi's Seventh Book – and the

---

[97] Gallico, 'La *lettera amorosa* di Monteverdi e lo stile rappresentativo', 287–302, p. 287.

[98] *Recital I (for Cathy)* was written for the singer Cathy Berberian and premiered on 27 April 1972 in Lisbon at the Calouste Gulbenkian Foundation auditorium. The *lettera amorosa* of Monteverdi is paired with a quotation from the *Lamento della ninfa* from the Eighth Book (1638). See Metzer, *Quotation and Cultural Meaning in Twentieth-Century Music*, pp. 219–20.

[99] See Lucienne Cantaloube-Ferrieu, 'Du chant au chant', 66–73 (p. 66, and p.73, 2n).

[100] There were two other prints of *L'amorosa ambasciatrice*, also in Vicenza in the same year 1612: One by Giacomo Cescato and the other Bortolamio de' Santi. The texts of all three are identical. In the 1612 print the poem is dedicated to one 'Signor Fabio Zogiano'. See Achillini, *L'amorosa ambasciatrice idilio del m. ill. & eccellentiss. signore C.A.*, pp. 7–14.

[101] See Schrade, *Monteverdi: Creator of Modern Music*, p. 291.

famous lament of Arianna from the eponymous opera of 1608. The print versions of Achillini's *lettera* are of varying lengths, none of which matches Monteverdi's text perfectly. The earliest print of 1612 gives an extended version of the poem, 198 verses in *versi sciolti*, while the text which appeared in Achilini's collected *Poesie*, dedicated in 1632 to the Duke of Parma Odoardo Farnese, is shortened to 141.[102] The additional verses that distinguish these versions of 'Se i languidi miei sguardi' fall within the middle section of the poem, most of which were cut in Monteverdi's monodic setting.

The earliest iteration of the text identifies the poem as an *idilio* with the title *l'amorosa ambasciatrice* ('the amorous ambassador') accompanied by a lengthy *argomento* describing the following epistolary situation.[103] A wandering poet seeks to inform his beloved of his amorous passion, knowing how true it is that such an ignited desire prohibits the tongue from expressing that which he imagines: 'l'imaginato concetto'. Instead, 'he took the pen into his hands, tracing [*lineando*] the beloved beauties, and shading [i.e., in ink] his pains, making the simple paper the happy messenger of his torments'.[104] The latter version of the text, first printed in Achillini's collected *Poesie* of 1632, also identifies the poem as the contents of a letter but with a briefer scenario; according to that inscription the poem is written by a 'Cavalier impatient on account of his delayed nuptials, writes this letter to his most beautiful lady'.[105] The poem is divided, roughly, into three different sections bookended by introductory and concluding passages. The parts correspond to three major parts of the lady's anatomy: her hair, her eyes, and her mouth. Monteverdi cuts out most of the latter two-thirds of the poem, choosing to focus on the poetic convolutions of the lady's golden tresses. That golden locks can do the 'work' of eros hearkens back to Acontius's letter from Ovid's *Heroides*, seen in Section 1:

---

[102] The longest of all (199 verses) is preserved in a manuscript, almost certainly autograph, preserved in the Biblioteca Universitaria di Bologna (BUB, cod. ms. 2322, ff. 438ʳ–439ʳ). According to Angelo Colombo the autograph version is an intermediary between the earliest 1612 prints (198 verses) and the 1632 *Poesie* (141 verses; this redacted version is also included in later collected prints with the revised title *Rime e prose di Claudio Achillini* [Venice: Giunti e Baba, 1650]). Colombo's edition is based primarily on this autograph manuscript, with noted variants from the 1612 prints and a second manuscript copy: BUB, cod. ms. 2692, ff. 57ʳ–60ᵛ. He does not account for the copy in Romano's *Seconda raccolta* (1620 [1618]). See Achillini, *Poesie*, pp. 310–37. For a comparison between Monteverdi's text and the later, 141-line version of the text (included in Achillini's 1632 *Poesie*) see Privitera, 'Leggete queste note', pp. 237–46; this article is included in the facsimile of the 1632 collected *Poesie* of Achillini.

[103] Note that the 'ambassador' (i.e., the letter) is gendered feminine (i.e., *la lettera*).

[104] 'Vagando il Poeta con l'anima per le campagne delle amorose passioni, avido di notificare all'amato oggetto l'incendio del cuore, conoscendo per prova quanto è vero, che una accesa voglia non lascia esprimere l'imaginato concetto alla lingua; presa nelle mani la penna, và lineando le bellezze amate, & ombreggiando le sue pene, facendo che la semplice carta, felice messaggiera de' suoi tormenti riesca'. *L'amorosa ambasciatrice*, p. 7.

[105] 'Cavaliere impaziente delle tardate nozze, scrive alla sua bellissima Sposa questa lettera'.

'this is the work of your golden tresses', Ovid has Acontius write, 'and that ivory throat, and the hands which I pray to have clasp my neck'.[106]

There is another textual source that may also shed light on the musical genesis of this *lettera amorosa*: Achillini's text appeared, in nearly its longest form, in the second instalment of musico-poetic anthologies assembled by the elusive Remigio Romano. Next to nothing is known about Romano, but his collections, some of which contain *alfabeto* musical notation, purport to bring together texts intended for or already set as songs and arias. Although Roark Miller and Silke Leopold have written about how musical prints may have been important sources for Romano's texts, there are far too many examples in which Romano's collections predate or otherwise do not correspond with the poems given in printed music of the period.[107] How he acquired these poems and the nature of their musical life before and after is still largely unknown. The *Seconda raccolta di canzonette musicali* was printed in 1620 but bears a dedication dated 4 October 1618. Achillini's *lettera amorosa* is given in a section titled 'Amor antico scoperto' and is, though neither poet nor composer is named, fitted with the prefatory title: 'Lettera di spiritoso soggetto, data gratiosissimamente alla musica'.[108] Like nearly all the poems included in Romano's anthology, the rubric implies that the love letter had either already been set to music, or could have been otherwise sung as an aria. While it is possible Romano might be referring to Monteverdi's setting, and if the earlier dating of the piece prior to its publication in 1619 stands true, the question about how he would have known of the piece remains open. What is more, Romano's text does not fit exactly, neither in its structure nor orthographic details, with the text given either in Monteverdi's 1619 book or in the 1623 print alongside the lament of Arianna. Not only does Romano's text contain the lengthy middle section of the poem that was cut both in Monteverdi and in Achillini's *Poesie*, but it also has an additional passage which dates back only to the 1612 print *L'amorosa ambasciatrice*.[109] The only other printed musical setting which appeared around the time of Romano's *Seconda raccolta* is a *concertato* setting for five voices and violins by Biagio Marini from his *Madrigali et symfonie* of 1618 which includes the excerpt 'Chi quella bella bocca', a text that comes, perhaps significantly, from that very passage of the poem included by Romano but cut out in the later versions.[110]

---

[106] Ovid, *Heroides*, XX. 57–8, pp. 278–79.

[107] See Miller, 'New Information on the Chronology of Venetian Monody', pp. 22–33; and Leopold, 'Remigio Romano's Collection of Lyrics for Music', pp. 45–61.

[108] Romano, *Seconda raccolta di canzonette musicali*, pp. 101–107.

[109] Romano's text is not identical to the 1612 version which runs 199 verses to Romano's 190.

[110] The only other setting, to my knowledge, is one for six voices by Giovanni Battista Locatello from his *Primo libro de madrigali* (1628): It survives incomplete in GB-Lbl (B, bc) and I-Ma (T2). Locatello sets only the first ten lines of Achillini's poem. There is also a text, 'Voi pur, begl'occhi, sete', set by Barbara Strozzi (1651) that bears some similarity to a few lines from

Despite a plethora of unanswered questions about their origins, Romano's collections offer important clues about the circulation of poems set as madrigals, monodies, and arias. In addition to Achillini's epistle, there are several other *lettere amorose* which appear in these poetic anthologies. In the *Prima raccolta* of 1618 Romano includes 'Fornito ha 'l corso Aprile', a lengthy poem in rhyming couplets identified in its preface both as the contents of a letter, and as one which had been set to music 'with the most excellent *stile recitativo*'.[111] As with Achillini's 'Se i languidi miei sguardi', it is not clear to whose musical setting Romano is referring. In a letter to librettist Hercole Marliani from 9 April 1621, the tenor Francesco Rasi mentions a song, 'Fornito ha 'l corso Aprile', as paired in performance with the 'Lamento d'Andromeda', a passage from Monteverdi's lost opera of 1620 for which Marliani himself wrote the libretto.[112] That the lament from *Andromeda*, like that of *Arianna*, had a performance life outside its original dramatic contexts probably explains why the music survives at all, at least in the case of the latter.[113] It is not totally clear from Rasi's letter whether the piece in question is his own composition, nor if it is definitely the same *lettera amorosa* printed in Romano's collection. To complicate matters further, a text that begins 'Fornito ha 'l corso Aprile' appears in a Florentine manuscript from the middle of the seventeenth century containing various works by Ottavio Rinuccini.[114] The poem is supposedly one of three 'epistole amorose in verso sciolto' listed in a table of contents prefacing that part of the manuscript.[115] The line 'Fornito ha 'l corso Aprile' itself does appear in a similar kind of poem from Rinuccini's collected *Poesie* of 1622, 'Sparito è luglio ardente', but the two poems are otherwise totally different.[116] What the manuscript does match almost

---

Achillini's *lettera*, also from the section cut by Monteverdi; see v. 79, 102 and 103 as they correspond to the first stanza of Strozzi's text.

[111] Romano's preface reads: 'Nella partita della cosa amate fù chi lasciò scritto le seguenti note, che furono poscia ridotte alla Musica con eccellentissimo stile recitativo'; see Romano, *Prima raccolta di bellissime canzonette musicali*, p. 61. This collection was originally printed and dedicated in 1618, also by Salvadori.

[112] Francesco Rasi was a tenor active in Mantua from 1598 and famously premiered the role of Orfeo in Monteverdi's 1607 opera. The letter from Rasi to Marliani is preserved in Mantua (AG 1022, unnumbered; *Herla* C–2955) and is dated Good Friday (9 April) 1621. In the letter, Rasi is referring to a hypothetical performance by the Roman singer Ippolita Recupito of the lament of Andromeda, 'Fornito ha 'l corso Aprile', and 'many of my own madrigals'; he claims that he would be amazed to hear such a performance, considering how in demand he himself was. See Carter, 'Monteverdi, Early Opera and a Question of Genre', 1–34 (p. 34, 58n).

[113] Both Arianna and Andromeda lived on as pieces for virtuoso performance circles off the stage; see Carter, 'Monteverdi, Early Opera and a Question of Genre', pp. 33–34.

[114] Biblioteca Nazionale Centrale di Firenze, Magl. VII.902, ff. 97ʳ–97ᵛ.

[115] The list appears on 66ᵛ and has the initials A.C. at the bottom.

[116] The line 'Fornito ha 'l corso Aprile' appears the middle of a lengthy poem, 'Sparito è luglio ardente', in Ottavio Rinuccini's *Poesie* (Florence: Giunti, 1622), pp. 173–76. The poem evokes the name of Cosimo II de' Medici, Grand Duke of Tuscany and addresses, on one occasion, his spouse Maria Maddalena of Austria (m. 1608): 'Credilo, Maddalena | credilo, e rasserena'. The line 'Fornito ha 'l

exactly is the *lettera amorosa* 'Fornito ha 'l corso Aprile' given in Romano's *Prima raccolta* of 1618, a book that also includes the texts of Rinuccini's most famous lamentations set by Monteverdi: the Lament of Arianna (1608) and the *Lamento della ninfa* (pub. 1638).[117]

The case of 'Fornito ha 'l corso Aprile' illustrates the close connections, both poetic and musical, between love letters and laments. In performance as in print, *lettere amorose* have been paired with both dramatic and non-dramatic laments: in other words, both with extractions from large-scale dramatic works as in Monteverdi's laments for Arianna or Andromeda, and with stand-alone chamber pieces, as in the *Lamento della ninfa* or Sigismondo d'India's chamber laments discussed in Section 4. The aforementioned Florentine manuscript also includes the libretto for Rinuccini's *Il Narciso* – a *favola in musica* considered but not set by Monteverdi – along with various other poems. The selections from Rinuccini seem eclectic – a libretto, dialogues, *canzonette*, *versi sciolti*, *balli*, etc. – but one thread that holds many of them together is a connection to Monteverdi, despite being copied around 1640. Furthermore, the other *epistola amorosa* included in this manuscript is none other than 'Se pur destina e vòle', Monteverdi's *partenza amorosa*, whose attribution to Rinuccini rests on this source alone.[118] The rationale for pairing Monteverdi's setting of Rinuccini's lament of Arianna with both the *partenza* 'Se pur destina e vòle' and Achillini's *lettera amorosa* is therefore cast in a new light, one that helps explain the designation 'in genere rappresentativo' given to them. Although the 1623 print certainly extended the popularity of Monteverdi's famous lament by including two more pieces for solo voice, there are nevertheless substantial connections between their respective texts.

Letters and laments tend to share similar subject matter, psychological pacing, and musical disposition. They trace a kind of cerebral narrative inspired by the physical absence and imagined presence of the beloved. They illustrate,

---

corso Aprile' appears on p. 176 not long after a reference to the famous opening line of Rinuccini's lament of Arianna, 'Lasciatemi morire', set in the same year, 1608, by Monteverdi. The implication is that Monteverdi himself may also have set the text though the music does not survive.

[117] The only difference in the case of 'Fornito ha 'l corso Aprile' is that in Romano's text the name of the beloved is Filli, not Cloride, as it appears in the manuscript. Curiously, the name 'Margerita' is written into the margin right next to Cloride's name (BNCF, Magl. VII 902, f. 97^r). In Romano's *Prima raccolta* (1618), Rinuccini is not listed as the author of 'Lasciatemi morire', the lament of Arianna 'registrato per eccelenza a stile recitativo di Musica', nor of 'Non havea Febo ancora', the *lamento della ninfa* set as a chamber piece in Monteverdi's *Madrigali guerrieri, et amorosi* (1638); see Romano, *Prima raccolta* (1622; originally published 1618), pp. 72–74 and 86–87.

[118] The poem appears on ff. 99^v–100^r of BNCF, Magl. VII 902. See Tomlinson, 'Music and the Claims of Text', 565–89 (p. 580, 23n). The table of contents on 66^r lists 'Epistole amorose in verso sciolto no. 3' though it is not clear which poem is supposed to be the third *lettera amorosa*, in addition to 'Fornito ha 'l corso Aprile' and 'Se pur destina e vòle'. One possibility may be a significantly briefer poem on 103^r with similar sentiments: 'Crudel tu voi partire' which is a *partenza* which both accuses the beloved and mourns their loss.

in other words, the dramatic and non-dramatic dimensions of the so-called *genere rappresentativo*. There are, however, important differences between laments and *lettere amorose*, even with their shared histories in performance and in print. Not only is the *lettera amorosa* unassociated with a particular dramatic context, but also it can be distinguished by the two musico-poetic mechanisms – sensory and perspectival – outlined in Section 1.

First, the poetic perspective of laments is, at least fundamentally, unambiguous: Arianna may address different people and entities in sporadic and unclear ways, but we are always certain that it is she who 'speaks' through the music. This is not the case in love letters where the voice of the writer may or may not be ventriloquized by the reader. Second, the sensory oscillation between visual and aural (i.e., between inanimate and animate), while shared by both letters and laments, is much more literal and pronounced when the words of a document become transformed into a musical performance. The sensory implications for the manipulation of time and temporality are also different in this sense. Arianna may conflate her memories with her experience in the present, but her words now are spoken, as it were, in real time. What is more, the words of lamenting characters tend, in dramatic contexts, to be overheard by witnesses functioning within the story. In the operatic version of Arianna's lament, the heroine's words are punctuated by a chorus of fishermen who have just rescued her from suicide; likewise in *Il ritorno d'Ulisse in patria* Penelope's lament is overheard by her nurse Ericlea.[119] The words of a letter do not represent an in-the-moment stream of emotional consciousness: they were composed in the past and are linked to the present through the written word. The conceit of the sung letter is that, as we have seen, it presents atemporal words through a temporal medium. If the words of a letter can function as a sort of soliloquy in performance, they are overheard not by other sympathetic characters in the story and certainly not by their intended recipient; they are considered only at a remove by listeners who are decidedly outside of the story.

Monteverdi's *lettera* and *partenza amorosa* are often considered together. They were both chosen for the 1623 Arianna print, and, in the Seventh Book of 1619, they are given a similar rubric: 'in genere rappresentativo e si canta senza battuta'.[120] This has been taken to mean that they are chamber monodies for solo voice in the so-called 'representative' genre, sung accordingly without the gestural

---

[119] The version of Arianna's lament in the 1623 print alongside the *lettera amorosa* has the fishermen omitted; as a chamber lament and divorced from its dramatic context Arianna's address is more generalized towards the absent Theseus and (perhaps) the audience of listeners. It is in this sense much more like a *lettera amorosa* although there is little doubt that she speaks in her own voice, unmediated by the written word. I am grateful to Tim Carter for this observation; see Carter, *Monteverdi's Musical Theatre*, pp. 207–11.

[120] Complete texts and translations are found in Online Appendices 3.2 and 3.3.

beating of time.[121] Filippo Vitali used the same phrase to preface his own *lettera amorosa*, 'Misero e pur convien, occhi crudeli', seen below. Though the poet of that text is unknown, this lengthy epistle is in many ways a clear nod to Monteverdi, not only through the shared designation, but because Vitali included it in a collection conspicuously named after Monteverdi's Seventh Book: *Concerto: Madrigali et altri generi di canti ... libro primo* (1629).[122]

Despite the shared designation *in genere rappresentativo*, there are subtle but significant stylistic and perspectival distinctions between Monteverdi's *lettera* and *partenza* which suggest that the latter is not, strictly speaking, a *lettera amorosa* at all. While the 1623 Arianna print calls each of them 'lettera amorosa', the original 1619 Seventh Book reserves that title for Achillini's 'Se i languidi miei sguardi' alone and specifies that Rinuccini's 'Se pur destina e vòle' is instead a *partenza amorosa*. The extent to which Monteverdi was directly involved with the publication of the 1619 book, or not in the case of the 1623, may not entirely explain this, but the difference in approach to musical and poetic voice suggests that the composer nevertheless drew a subtle yet intriguing distinction between the two poems.[123]

If on the surface the two pieces seem similar, the details tell a different story. Although Rinuccini's *partenza*, like the *lettera*, relates the woes of a lover to his beloved, it is actually a very different kind of poem. Achillini's *lettera amorosa* is written as a long string of *versi sciolti* whereas Rinuccini's text, like the aforementioned 'Fornito ha 'l corso Aprile', is written in rhyming couplets, or *rime baciate*, as opposed to Achillini's *settenari*, and is perhaps closer in style to Chiabrera than to Marino, practically speaking.[124] The more substantial difference, however, runs along the same sensory and perspectival lines outlined above, namely that the

---

[121] Monteverdi makes the distinction in his instruction for 'Non havea Febo ancora' from the Eighth Book, also called the *Lamento della Ninfa*, on a text by Rinuccini. According to Monteverdi the three male voices should sing 'al tempo dela mano' while the solo soprano 'va cantato a tempo del' affetto del animo, e non quello dela mano'. See Gallico, 'La 'lettera amorosa' di Monteverdi', p. 299. It is worth pointing out that the gestures of keeping time were not synonymous with performance gestures in general. The title page of Monteverdi's Eighth Book instructs readers that pieces 'in genere rappresentativo' are brief episodes between songs without action ('episodii fra i canti senza gesto'). The gestural beating of time (distinguished from the action 'gesto' perhaps implied in the *genere rappresentativo*) is very commonly seen in contemporary paintings which depict singers performing from partbooks.

[122] Similar is another love letter by Orazio Tarditi, 'Questa carte ch'io sparsi' from his *Madrigali a doi, tre, e quattro voci in concerto ... libro secondo* (1633) which is given the title 'lettera amorosa in stile recitativo a voce sola'.

[123] Gary Tomlinson has also underscored the distinction between the *lettera* and the *partenza* albeit on different grounds. His reading was based primarily on the difference in quality he saw between Achillini's and Rinuccini's texts; because the *lettera* was an 'emotionally frigid' Marinist piece Monteverdi responded accordingly by setting it to 'lifeless declamation', the *partenza*, as supposedly more emotionally complex poem, elicited a stronger response from the composer. See Tomlinson, 'Music and the Claims of Text', pp. 580–85.

[124] Tomlinson calls 'Se pur destina e vòle' 'a frottola of a sort written a century earlier by Benivieni ... revived by a number of Florentine poets of the early century'. Interestingly, he compares it to

lettera is about writing and reading, while the *partenza* is about speaking and listening. This has consequences when the poems are sung. Monteverdi's *lettera amorosa* is cleffed for soprano (C1) while the poem itself is in the male voice: the performance seems to suggest the reading of the letter by its recipient, not its writer. The music represents the words of one through the voice of another. Such a role reversal – a woman singing the emotions of a man – was censured as lacking in decorum by the Florentine theorist Giovanni Battista Doni (discussed in the Prologue), who called the piece 'more capricious than reasonable' not considering, perhaps, the possibility of a performance by a castrato singer.[125]

Unlike Doni, however, Monteverdi may not have seen such ambiguity of perspective as a problem even if his choice of clef does suggest a specific vocal tessitura. As seen in Section 2, a musical performance of a letter does not necessarily resolve the question of who is speaking: the writer, the recipient, the letter itself, or a dynamic ventriloquizing of all three. The *partenza* on the other hand, though also written from the perspective of the male lover, is set by Monteverdi in tenor clef (C4); the performance may represent the speech of the person uttering their own words. While the author of the *lettera* asks his beloved to read these words ('leggete queste note') and see himself reflected there ('qui sotto scorgerete'), Rinuccini's lover instead asks her to listen ('ascolta') and to hear his words ('odi le voci estreme'). The mood of the *partenza* is in this sense closer to a lament, in which the wronged characters of mythology call after their departed lovers and request responses in vain: 'Ahi, che non pur rispondi' asks Arianna of Theseus in Rinuccini's lament for her set by Monteverdi. Similar meditations on hearing, speaking, and listening are likewise found in the laments for Dido by Sigismondo d'India; a monody with text and music by the composer; and another lament for Arianna by Giambattista Marino, 'Misera, e chi m'ha tolto', set to music in 1623 by Pellegrino Possenti.

The words in the *partenza* may be ineffectual, but they are said nevertheless. The *lettera* begins, by contrast, with the admission that spoken words pale in

---

another of Rinuccini's poems – 'Sparito è luglio ardente', discussed above – which he does not name but also calls a *frottola*. See Tomlinson, 'Music and the Claims of Text', pp. 580–81.

[125] Doni, who never totally clears up the confusion regarding the stylistic characteristics of the *genere rappresentativo*, calls both 'Se i languidi miei sguardi' and 'Se pur destina e vòle' *lettere*: 'Ma l'invenzione delle *Lettere* ha più del capriccioso, che del ragionevole: perciocchè benchè siano state raccontate, come s'ha da credere, a qualche Dama, che sapesse cantare, e sonare; tuttavia non pare che abbia del buono, che quello, che doverebbe dire, o cantare l'amante, la Dama stessa lo cantasse'; 'the invention of the *Lettere* has more of the capricious than the reasonable: For although both are recounted, as we are to believe, to some lady who knows how to sing and play, however it does not seem good that that which the lover should say or sing should be sung by a woman herself (trans. Carter, in Fabbri, *Monteverdi*, p. 167); Doni, *Trattato della musica scenica* (1633–5), cap. XI, in *Lyra Barberina*, ii, p. 26. See also Gallico, 'La 'lettera amorosa' di Monteverdi', pp. 287–88 and Privitera 'Leggete queste note', p. 246.

comparison to the mediated, refracted words written in a letter: 'If my languid glances, if my interrupted sighs, if my halting words have not thus far been able, o my lovely idol, to tell you of my faithful ardour; read these words, believe this letter, this letter, in which, under the guise of ink, I distilled my heart' (see text and translation in online Appendix 3.2). Monteverdi follows the breathless *settenari* that open Achillini's *lettera* with 'disconcerting regularity,'[126] for the lines are just that: disconcerting, hesitant, and interrupted. The recipient musically reads her beloved's words, or rather, his incomplete and halting words, in a manner that suggests that she too is uncertain how to express these ventriloquized emotions. Words not being enough, the writer turns to the letter itself, the more faithful mirror of his inner self, which he bids her to read and believe: 'Here below you will see those inner thoughts which with steps of love flow through my soul' (vv. 11–14). Only by looking at the paper will she be able to see him truly, the paper into which he has distilled his own heart by means of the liquid ink. The poet transforms the complicated emotions of unrequited love into physical objects – the letter itself, and later golden tresses – thus creating an unexpected link between the immaterial conflicts of the heart and the physical qualities of the material world. Monteverdi's musical distillation of Achillini's words gives the lady, the recipient, the opportunity through her performance to retrace and remould this alchemical transformation of heart into letter. The comparatively static, almost frustrated opening musical line on 'Se i languidi miei sguardi' gives way to a spectacularly ornate free-flowing melisma on the word 'cor' ('heart') (Example 5). If the opening words, appropriately, seem to convey an emotional frigidity, then Monteverdi's music serves to thaw them, reversing the trajectory of animate to inanimate that created the letter in the first place.

The opening of the *partenza* evokes the senses differently. The lover bids his beloved to listen not to his written words, but to those about to be uttered by his own tongue: 'Listen, my dear goddess, to what the cold and trembling tongue of a disconsolate lover may say again [*ridire*] amongst such great suffering' (vv. 4–8; online Appendix 3.3). In the *partenza*, the aural sense is directly referred to in the text itself whereas in the *lettera* it is created only through the performance of Monteverdi's music. The visual plays a role in both, albeit to two different ends. If in the *lettera* the author implores his lady to look upon the letter as his soul's proxy, the speaker of the *partenza* asks her to contemplate (*rimira*) a tear, elicited by his words, as it travels away from her eyes towards her snowy breast, a foreshadowing of his own departure (vv. 14–19). The sense of sight is not referred to obliquely or figuratively as in the *lettera*, but literally, as a window to the soul that circumvents the need for words, which are ultimately imperfect impediments in amorous

---

[126] Tomlinson, 'Music and the Claims of Text', p. 581.

Example 5 Claudio Monteverdi, 'Se i languidi miei sguardi' (*Lettera amorosa*), mm. 1–11

communication. Later in the *partenza,* the speaker addresses not his lady, but a set of eyes: 'Lumi, voi che vedeste' (v. 41). These are not the beloved's eyes, however, but rather his own. He asks them for aid ('a voi dimando aiuto') for if his lady looks upon them, they would be able to tell her of his bitter anguish far more effectively than any of his words could (Example 6). In pairing the *lettera* and *partenza* and setting them both in *genere rappresentativo*, Monteverdi therefore makes a neat juxtaposition of the senses – seeing and hearing words both read and spoken – through an affective monodic language. In these pieces the *genere rappresentativo* is not, to paraphrase Claudio Gallico, a mechanical application of the recitative style, nor is it a generic or generally dramatic disposition; rather, it is a very particular 'musical condition', a mode both moving and communicative, which can be used to represent both the internalized meditation and externalized theatricality of impassioned emotion.[127]

---

[127] Gallico, 'La *lettera amorosa* di Monteverdi', p. 301; 'Sì una condizione musicale specifica, in rapporto con parole ricche di affetto: quella condizione musicale commossa e communicative,

Example 6 Monteverdi, 'Se pur destina e vòle' (*Partenza amorosa*), mm. 43–55

The sensory transformation within and between the *lettera* and *partenza* is further complemented by Monteverdi's approach to poetic voice and perspective. This does not happen solely through the choice of clef and range as we have seen – the fact that the *lettera* can be sung by its recipient and the *partenza* by a departing lover – it also has to do with the way Monteverdi parses the poetry. Both the *lettera* and *partenza* have long texts compared to most pieces included in madrigal books. The ways the texts are musically divided are not

---

che sostanzia in Monteverdi tutto un diagramma di tipi compositivi, disposti fra il puro meditativo e il vero e proprio teatro'.

just tools for practicality, they reveal how pronouns of poetic address as well as poetic themes influenced the composer's formal rendering of the texts. Silke Leopold has pointed out that the cadential plan of Monteverdi's *lettera* seems roughly to follow the unequal but grammatically separated syntactical units of Achillini's text.[128] As the translations in online Appendices 3.2 and 3.3 show, Monteverdi also parses the texts of his *lettera* and *partenza* with fermatas which usually correspond to grammatical full stops but occasionally do not. This seems much more consciously and conspicuously done in the *partenza* in whose middle section two- or three-line segments are isolated by fermatas from the adjacent verses. In the *lettera* the fermatas not only correspond to poetic themes, but they also mark the places where Monteverdi made cuts to the text, as discussed above. In both cases, however, the fermatas function both practically – places of rest give a formal profile to a lengthy text – and semantically – they mark the perspectival shifting that defines, in different ways, the eroticism of each text. In the *lettera* this manifests a triangulation between author, recipient, and listener, whereas in the *partenza* it represents the fragmented inner psyche of the departing lover.

In the *lettera*, the first juncture Monteverdi marks with a fermata is at line 22, 'che di vostra beltà preda e trofeo'. This is the moment when the author stops speaking to the recipient (i.e., the performer of the letter) and turns to the primary conceit of the poem: the beloved's golden tresses that have bound him in love. Achillini marks the juncture with a clear change in address: 'A voi mi volgo, o chiome'.[129] Although the subsequent sections are all addressed to the golden hair – in other words, the performer sings to her own hair in another's voice – they each focus on a particular aspect of their binding powers. The golden bonds are the means by which Fate spins the lover's destiny (vv. 23–33); they are fiery sparks that, contrary to actual fire, descend instead of ascend (vv. 34–43); they create a labyrinth from which the beloved's soul cannot hope to escape (vv. 44–54); and finally they are a beautiful rain of gold that in precious storms bathes the alabaster shores of the lady's brow and, paradoxically, burn the lover's heart in tempests of love (vv. 55–67). This last section, at 'Dolcissimi legami', is not technically sectioned off with fermatas although one wonders whether that might have been intended, as the image conveyed is rather different from the labyrinth that precedes it.[130] The music at

---

[128] Leopold, *Al modo d'Orfeo*, pp. 163–65.
[129] For deixis in the operatic context see Calcagno, 'Monteverdi's *parole sceniche*', para. 2.1–2.4.
[130] There are in fact several discrepancies in the orthography and layout of the various prints that raise the possibility that a fermata might have been intended here but was accidentally omitted; see footnotes in the text and translation in online Appendix 3.2.

'Dolcissimi legami' is also reminiscent of the opening gesture 'Se i languidi miei sguardi'.

The most significant juncture, however, comes after the final section (v. 67): the place where Monteverdi cut out the majority of Achillini's poem. There are several possible explanations for the intervention. It is possible Monteverdi wished to focus on the more musically evocative of the images: the dynamic *concettismo* of the tresses was more visceral than the meditations on the eyes and mouth with which Achillini's poem continues. Perhaps Monteverdi wished to avoid some of the specificity of the middle part of the poem, in which particular circumstances are related and the beloved's name, Berenice, is revealed. Or maybe he simply found the poem to be too long. But in retaining the last section of the text, which is also the very end of Achillini's letter, Monteverdi concludes the piece with another perspectival shift that is significant because it is necessary to the epistolary of the poem. 'Ma già l'ora m'invita' shifts the address once again: the singer now 'speaks' to the letter itself in the voice of her lover. But this time the formal address of the opening 'voi' gives way to the familiar 'tu' suggesting an even greater artificial 'distance' between the author of the words and the singer who utters them. 'But now the hour beckons me, o faithful messenger of my affections, dear love letter, to divide you now from my pen' ('dalla penna *ti* divida omai'). The writer may address the letter itself in informal terms when direct and open communication with his beloved is not possible; he tells it to go ('Vanne') and nestle itself in her breast: the place he cannot go.[131] When she sings the words though, he may have it both ways: she gives voice to his words addressed to the letter which, in turn, creates audible closeness by way of grammatical distance.

This final stanza – the moment when the epistolary nature of the *lettera* is confirmed in performance – brings us back to the central issue of whether listeners are actually privy to the letter's contents. Surely the final stanza of Monteverdi's *lettera amorosa* at 'Ma già l'hora m'invita' is a text of which the recipient cannot possibly have sight: these are not his words to his lady but rather parting words to the letter itself prior to its departure. If that is the case, then the hypothesis that the singer 'stands in' for the recipient and represents her voice reading the words sent to her does not seem to work. A partial solution, as Tim Carter suggests, is to interpret the performance as the letter

---

[131] In Frescobaldi's 'Vanne o carta amorosa' (*Secondo libro d'arie musicali*, Florence, 1630), another heavily redacted idyll by the poet Girolamo Preti, the letter writer also has the letter do most of the 'talking'; he instructs the letter not only to go to his beloved but to tell her about his feelings. Preti's text was published in his *Idilli e Rime*, dedicated to Ascanio Pio di Savoia: librettist for Monteverdi's five lost intermedi that he composed to accompany Tasso's *Aminta* at the 1628 wedding festivities at Parma. Ascanio was nephew to the Ferrarese impresario Enzo Bentivoglio.

itself 'speaking', a situation that would make a great deal of sense not only with the majority of Achillini's text but also with Monteverdi's choice of clefs and parsing of the text. But the performance, I would argue, still manages to preserve enough ambiguity to allow listeners a variety of possible interpretations. As we saw in the epistolary madrigals of Marino, the genre allowed for the kind of conceits in which epistolary communication can itself be a conversation with an inanimate object. It is possible that the final stanza of Monteverdi's *lettera amorosa* is in fact the end of a letter, but it is also possible that it is not. The singer, like the listeners, has some agency here to interpret and reinterpret. The deliberate concealment, or rather the partial concealment of the contents of a letter was, after all, one of the most appealing aspects of Dutch letter painting (see Prologue). The *lettera amorosa* is attractive not because it promises a 'solution' to a curiosity but because it is itself a representational curiosity.

In the middle section of the *partenza,* Monteverdi's parsing of the text has rather different consequences than in the *lettera amorosa*. The fermatas mark off sections of irregular length that in this passage convey perspectival shifting occurring *within* the narrator's fragmented psyche. At 'Vita del la mia vita' (v. 30), the narrator at first expresses his anxiety in bidding farewell to his beloved whom he addresses directly and informally: 'A *te* non dico a Dio'. Although the following line of Achillini's text continues logically, in giving the reason why the narrator fears his own imminent departure, Monteverdi isolates these two lines by placing a fermata at 'a Dio'. Monteverdi's parsing does, however, make sense when one considers that the perspective of address changes in the lines that follow: the narrator is no longer addressing his beloved but rather, retrospectively, himself. 'A te' is replaced by 'a me' as he expresses his wish to take leave of himself, 'A me, vo' dir a Dio | a me, che triste e solo', for his heart and soul remain with his beloved. What seems to have caught Monteverdi's ear in this passage is the way in which an introspective declaration of self-loathing plays wittily on the resulting grammatical parallel of Rinuccini's text. The subsequent passage at 'Lumi, voi che vedeste' (v. 41), briefly mentioned above, has yet another perspectival shift that Monteverdi musically indicates: the lover finally addresses his own eyes ('a voi, tremante e muto | a voi, dimando aiuto') to complete the trio of object pronouns. Monteverdi aurally links every address – 'a te', 'a me', 'a voi' – with an anacrusis figure rising both in pitch and intensity (Example 7). These supplications seek to represent the internal conflict of the lover. They are conspicuous not only visually – in that Rinuccini places them at the beginnings of lines – but also audibly – in that Monteverdi musically emphasizes the repetition of the pronouns in order to connect and delineate different parts of the lengthy text. In the case of the

Example 7 Monteverdi, *Partenza amorosa*, mm. 32–42

partenza, the shifting of perspective represents the lover's inner turmoil while also deliberately delaying the dreaded moment of parting. The perspectival shifting is therefore also temporal, and functions in this sense as a mechanism of eroticism: the lover seems to turn from one thing to another so as to prolong the desirous moment which cannot be prolonged. The eroticism of the *partenza* is thus in the desired but impossible slowing of time. Rinuccini's direct reference to the slowing of Phoebus's hand (i.e., time) upon hearing the beloved's laments – 'Deh, con più lenta mano'(v. 20) – lends both a literal

Example 8 Monteverdi, *Lettera amorosa*, mm. 23–39

and figurative meaning to Monteverdi's affective instruction that the piece be sung 'senza battuta'.

Achilllini's *lettera* also plays on this kind of anaphora, although much more obliquely and less regularly than in Rinuccini's *partenza*. Here the scorned lover addresses the beloved's hair, the ensnaring metallic tresses that make the central *concetto* of the whole poem. He 'speaks' to her hair ('A voi mi volgo, o chiome'; 'voi, voi, o capelli d'oro') but the speech is only sounded through her own voice. The lady's blond tresses are described as chains of precious metals that have trapped the letter-writer, presumably in love. The capricious address 'a voi', 'voi, voi', 'voi pur' is repeated several times; Monteverdi sets each repetition with clear upward intervallic leaps in the melodic line, now a fourth, now a fifth or a sixth (Example 8). Achillini uses this kind of repetition to transform a situation of unrequited love into a physical object – a golden chain – thus creating an unexpected link between the immaterial conflicts of the heart and the physical qualities of the material world. In this middle section of the *lettera,* the poetic address does not change, grammatically speaking, as it does in the *partenza*. But the repetitive insistence, both poetically and musically, on the pronouns and their repetition in performance creates an ambiguity in the way they are heard and understood. Monteverdi's setting serves to remind the listener that the peculiar vocality of this piece results in a perspectival triangulation between the letter-writer, the recipient, and the audience itself: all three may stand in as 'voi' depending on who is reading and who is listening.

4 *Lettera amorosa* in the Seventeenth Century

Claudio Achillini's *lettera amorosa* owes a great deal to the influence of his older contemporary Giambattista Marino, the poet whose name is almost synonymous with the poetics of the seventeenth century. In addition to the witty and concise madrigal love letters seen in Section 2, Marino also composed a lengthy *lettera amorosa* much closer in its structure to those of Achillini and Preti. The poem is as virtuosic as it is thought-provoking, further illustrating the idiosyncrasies of epistolary poetry seen so far. Although the poem might have been largely unknown in musical circles – it was thought to have remained unpublished even at the poet's death in 1625 – it did garner two musical settings by Monteverdi's rival Sigismondo d'India.[132] The earliest of D'India's settings, 'Scherniscimi, crudele', has a variant opening line and appeared in the *Musiche libro terzo* of 1618, while a longer version, 'Torna dunque, deh torna', follows more closely the printed version of Marino's text and appeared in the *Musiche libro quarto* of 1621.[133] The proximity between poet and composer in Turin may account for D'India's having access to early and unpublished versions of Marino's poetry.[134] The *lettera amorosa* by Marino was published in a collection of his own letters and in later editions came to bear the title 'Alla sua donna'; it was included in the second edition of Marino's correspondence published in 1628 by the Venetian publisher Giacomo Sarzina.[135] In this edition, the *lettera amorosa* has its own brief preface that begins 'Si scusa il poeta' written in the voice of the poet.[136] The preface gives a synopsis of the lengthy text to follow: the poet writes to his lady apologizing for his weakness caused by the hold that she has over him, curses her infidelity, decides to forgive her capricious nature for it is common to all women, and resolves to die willingly, should her eyes wish it.[137]

---

[132] That Marino composed the letter during his stay in Turin (1611–15) is hinted at by his reference in the text to being surrounded by the Alps ('quest'Alpi che intorno | fanno al la bella Italia argine e muro') and to the town of Moncenisio in Piedmont ('ch'imbianchan del Moncise il capo alpino'), Marino, *Lettere*, p. 591.

[133] Garavaglia, *Sigismondo D'India 'drammaturgo'*, p. 101.

[134] This was likely the case for D'India's early settings of Marino's epic poem *L'Adone*; see Giles, 'Giambattista Marino's *L'Adone*' 419–40.

[135] The first edition, which was published in Venice by Francesco Baba one year prior in 1627, does not include the *lettera amorosa*. See Russo, 'Le lettere del Marino e la cultura di primo Seicento', p. 661, 1n.

[136] Marino, *Lettere del Caval. Marino*, pp. 265–68.

[137] This preface, 'Si scusa il Poeta', is not found in all prints of Marino's *Lettere* (there is a different preface containing more or less the same summary in the 1673 printing for example also published by Francesco Baba); the text from the 1628 edition reads: 'Si scusa il Poeta in questa lettera d'Amore, che se diffetto è in lui, ò mancamento, avviene per il predominio eccessivo, sopra di lui, che tiene la sua Diva, che violentemente lo agita, che però la prega, che favoreuoli sia, come li fù un tempo, e la fede data è giurata, richiede, che non si trova in Terra, nè in Cielo, ò nell'Inferno, e ingelosito per sua Antitesi crudelissima: E il tutto scorge, che Amore à gli occhi d'Argo: E più li piace, che lo tassi d'infedeltà, però la scusa come Donna solita à simil mancamenti, come serpi

It appears, however, that the earliest printed edition of this *lettera amorosa* was not in any collection of poetry devoted exclusively to Marino and nor, apparently, was it posthumous. The text of Marino's *lettera amorosa* first appeared, albeit without acknowledgement, in the *Terza raccolta di bellissime canzoni* of Remigio Romano, first printed in Vicenza by Savaldori in 1620.[138] As in Romano's earlier anthologies (see Section 3), the *lettera amorosa* appears alongside a plethora of texts that were, according to their compiler, sung as arias and *canzonette*. Although this alone does not necessarily mean that D'India could not have gotten his texts directly from the poet – there is, after all, a different first line in his 1618 setting that does not match any printed version of the poetry – it does suggest that the text, in whole or in part, was circulating widely in manuscript and even amongst musicians long before it was published in Marino's collected letters.

The close relationship between letters and laments both in performance and in print is brought to bear in D'India's books of *Musiche* from 1621 and 1623. In addition to the monodic setting of Marino's *lettera amorosa*, the former contains laments for Orpheus and Apollo with words by the composer, while the latter has a set of laments for Dido, Jason, and Olympia, again on *versi sciolti* written, presumably, by D'India himself. That D'India may have written such lamentations for solo voice in response, at least in part, to Monteverdi is certainly plausible. The chamber lament of Dido in particular bears musical similarities to Monteverdi's lament for Arianna and led Tim Carter to conclude that the affinities are 'at times verging on direct quotation'.[139] In addition to a passage on the line 'E tu, cor mio, se privo | de la tua vita sei, come sei vivo? | O de l'anima mia spento desio' discussed by Carter,[140] D'India replicates in his *Lamento di Didone* the most recognizable musical gesture of Monteverdi's famous lament. D'India sets the line 'Ahi, che finir mi sento!' with exactly the same musical gesture – albeit fragmented with emphatic rests – as the opening minor second of Arianna's lament by Monteverdi, 'Lasciatemi morire' (Examples 9 and 10).[141] But the poetry of Marino's *lettera amorosa*, even in

---

velenosi, tuttavia è costante, in amarla, ancora che crudele, che se li occhi suoi desiderano là di lui morte, morirà vòlentieri. Pur che pianto da lei sia la sua morte', Marino, *Lettere* p. 265.

[138] The poem appears in the 1622 reprint of Romano's *Terza raccolta* with the title 'Lettera amorosa' but without acknowledgement of Marino as author (this seems to be common for Romano). See Romano, *Terza raccolta di bellissime canzoni*, pp. 6–22. Marziano Guglielminetti's critical edition of Marino's letters does include the *lettera amorosa* but is based on the 1628 Sarzina print and does not mention the earlier Romano print. See Marino, *Lettere*, pp. 581–94.

[139] Carter, 'Intriguing Laments', pp. 32–69 (p. 40).

[140] This passage is identified and quoted by Carter, 'Intriguing Laments', p. 41; it corresponds with the line 'Son queste le corone | onde m'adorn'il crine | questi gli scettri sono | queste le gemme e gl'ori | lasciarmi in abbandono | a fera che mi strazi e mi devori?' from Rinuccini's text for Monteverdi's *Lamento d'Arianna*.

[141] This comes in bar 105 of John Joyce's edition; D'India, *Le Musiche a una e due voci, Libri I–V (1609–1623)*, p. 303.

Example 9 Monteverdi, 'Lamento d'Arianna' (1623), mm. 1–2

Example 10 Sigismondo d'India, 'Lamento di Didone', mm. 103–6

D'India's redacted version, is distinguished from lament texts in consisting of explicitly written words in an aural and temporal medium.

The complete text of Marino's *lettera amorosa* begins, as is typical, with a lover's supplication to his beloved, 'A te, che sola sei | dolce salute sua, manda salute | il più dolente e sconsolato core'. The language is in Marino's characteristically convoluted style, but is here surprisingly affecting, even charming. Having already given his lover the entirety of his being, the writer of the poem now offers her this letter: the only token of himself left that is at present properly his (online Appendix 4.1a). The play on pronouns here ('tuo'/ 'sua') may lead us to ask similar questions to those suggested by the performance of Monteverdi's settings of Achillini and Rinuccini (see Section 3). Is the letter, as a token of the writer, not also a reflection of the beloved? Is the mistaking of one for the other not a central characteristic of this kind of poetry in performance? In the opening passage, we find references to writing, paper, pens and cards: the kinds of physical indications of letter writing that were used in similar poems by Achillini, as we have seen, and by Girolamo Preti, the author of a *lettera amorosa* set by Frescobaldi in 1630.[142] The lover's character is initially a familiar one in the Petrarchan lyric tradition: the lovesick and self-deprecating poet, whose words are incapable of adequately praising his beautiful lady, dwells instead on his affliction. Even as the lady is raised onto the proverbial pedestal, Marino's letter begins 'a te' conspicuously in the informal address.

The predictable poetic self-deprecation of the opening lines does not last, however, because what starts as a supplication to an unattainable lady morphs into a literal and shocking accusation of infidelity: 'tu, che tanto ti mostri | instabile e sleale, | me condannar d'instabiltade ardisci?' (online Appendix 4.1b). Marino begins in the realm of recognizable poetic tropes – the perfect feminine beauty and the melancholic admirer – luring the reader into the classic and familiar 'at a distance' poetic veneration. He then destabilizes all expectations by transforming language that was metaphorical, and thus somewhat removed from reality, into a physical and painfully real account of betrayal. Whereas Petrarch languishes in love, hardly ever speaking to his ethereal Laura, Marino's letter-writer openly accuses his lover, dragging her abruptly down from the heavens to the physical world in order to show how unworthy she really is. The lines from Marino's *lettera amorosa* are not unlike those spoken by the wife of King Herod in the poet's *La strage degli innocenti* (1632), as she, in chilling excoriation, condemns her husband for the murder of their own child.[143]

The final section of the *lettera* presents another unsettling change in mood; despite his combative tone earlier in the poem, the writer now begs his lover to return to him in much more regimented and regular *settenari*. Beginning at 'Torna dunque, deh torna' the poem seems no longer addressed to the specific woman with whom the writer has a history, but is directed once more at the generic unattainable lady met at the opening of the letter (online Appendix 4.1c). Further, what was a comparatively elegant alternation of seven- and eleven-syllable *versi piani* is changed suddenly at the beginning of this passage to regular, somewhat breathless seven-syllable *settenari*. There is thus a discernable shift in both the subject and form at this point in the letter, one that proved a starting point for Sigismondo d'India's musical setting.

The psychological and emotional arc of the *lettera amorosa* is in this way symmetrical: the typical scorned lover and the perfect lady of the opening

---

[142] Another *lettera amorosa* – 'Questa pallida carta' for solo voice – is by the composer Giovanni Bettini (*fl.* 1616–24). The *lettera amorosa* of Bettini – whose text also plays on the senses of sight and hearing – is preserved in manuscript in Prague, CZ-Pnm Sign.II La 2 (no. 48), formerly in the Lobkowicz library at Roudnice. A transcription of the piece is found in Helena Tašnerová, 'Rukopisný sborník italské monodie z Lobkowiczké knihovny [A Manuscript of Italian Monody from the Lobkowicz Library]', (unpublished master's thesis, Charles University, 2009), p. 181. See also Carter, 'Bettini, Giovanni', Grove Music Online, 2001, accessed 5 December 2022.

[143] See the passages at the end of the fourth book of *La strage degli innocenti* where the wife of King Herod weeps for her dead child, accuses her husband and finally commits suicide: Marino, *La strage degli innocenti*; Marino, *The Massacre of the Innocents*, pp. 198–203.

passage are transformed into a man and woman of flesh and blood, only to be fossilized again as two ideals by the end of the poem. The reader/listener is initially astonished by the virtuosity with which the beloved is represented; they are then disillusioned in the discovery that what was ideal is physical and what seemed heavenly is earthly; and, finally, they accept that the artificial is as real as the natural. This is Marino's *meraviglia*, achieved in the *lettera amorosa* through a subversive presentation of traditional metaphors and poetic tropes.[144] By extension, the experience of hearing Marino's *lettera* performed as a musical piece enacts this same emotional engagement with artifice in real time and thus creates a musical analogue for the poem's *meraviglia*.

D'India's monodic setting of Marino's *lettera* skips most of the poem and begins with the supplication for the lover's return at the line 'Torna, dunque deh torna'. The mood of the text is therefore very unlike that achieved by a *lettera amorosa* by Filippo Vitali, seen below, whose anonymous text is focused almost entirely on accusations of betrayal by his unfaithful lady. In the composer's original print, the piece is prefaced by the title 'lettera amorosa del Cavalier Marino', given perhaps to solidify the connection between poet and composer since, as mentioned, the only printed version of the text that had appeared by this point did not give the poet's name. D'India's chosen passage is centred around the call for the lady's return to the lamenting lover. The plea of 'Torna!' that begins the piece comes back about halfway through the extracted passage of Marino's *lettera*, on the line 'Torna, torna e reintegra | questa parte di me lacera e manca' ('return, return and restore this part of me torn and lacking'; online Appendix 4.1d). D'India's version of the text varies slightly from Marino's and in this line the word 'manca' ('lacking') is replaced with 'stanca' ('tired') implying, curiously, that the piece of him which is missing is in fact weary (Example 11). While the supplication for the beloved to return is a refrain found in many lament texts, Monteverdi's lament for Penelope in the 1640 opera *Il ritorno d'Ulisse in patria* for example, the context of a letter written and read casts it in a rather different light.[145] The line immediately following refers specifically to the fact that this plea is written as much as it might be spoken: 'e tu vedrai per prova | se da bugiardo o da verace affetto | quanto parlo è prodotto e quanto scrivo' ('and you will see as proof if from deceitful or truthful feeling it is made, what

---

[144] Francesco Guardiani has suggested something similar in his study of Marino's *L'Adone*: 'La prima parte ha un tono positivo, quasi trionfalistico ("E così che si fa poesia" è il messaggio critico del poeta sotteso all'*enunciazione*): la metafora tradizionale assicura l'esattezza della rappresentazione di un sentimento ... La seconda parte esprime apprensione, perfino angoscia. Il poeta denuncia l'inaffidabilità della figurazione convenzionale, la sua falsità addirittura'; Guardiani, *La meravigliosa retorica dell'Adone di G.B. Marino*, p. 31.

[145] For a detailed discussion of Monteverdi's reconstruction of Penelope's lament see Rosand, *Monteverdi's Last Operas*, pp. 251–68.

Example 11 D'India, 'Torna dunque, deh torna', mm. 31–9

I say as much as what I write'). That piece of himself that is torn, 'questa parte de me lacera', is therefore not just a reference to the beloved herself, but also ostensibly to the letter, which is a true and material part of the lover's heart to which she may respond. The feelings produced ('se da bugiardo o da verace affetto') may in the epistolary context be as much his sent as hers received.

Although the declamatory style of D'India's *lettera* may complement the natural inflections of the text, in the opening passage the composer uses the percussive nature of recitation in a way that reflects the structure of the text more than it does the specific meaning of the words. In the passage following the initial lover's plea 'Torna dunque, deh torna', the stresses and inflections of the text that were so central to the ethos of recitative become secondary to a long and exasperated rising musical sequence. At the line 'gemma di questo seno' through to 'Stella ch'infondi e piovi', the singer begins in bar 9 on a c' – the lowest pitch of the piece so far – and continues their ascent via a series of applied dominants and quick repeated notes to culminate an octave and a fifth higher in bar 21 on a top g" (Example 12). Marino's regular *settenari* here convey increasingly frenzied permutations of the relatively impersonal compliments mentioned above. The semantic meaning of the words is less important than the building of energy and intensifying passion in the way each line seems to fall breathlessly into the next. Instead of focusing on the individual words themselves, D'India appropriately chose to express the text more abstractly, or

Example 12 D'India, 'Torna dunque, deh torna', mm. 1–22

artificially, by creating a seemingly endless chain of applied leading tones with no clear harmonic goal in the continuo, combined with a stressful ascent in the vocal part. The result in performance is both breathless and emotionally exasperating.

But whose emotions are these? D'India's *lettera amorosa* is notated with a C1 clef suggesting, as in Monteverdi's 'Se i languidi miei sguardi', that the singer is intended to be a soprano. Marino's *lettera* is likewise written from a male perspective – the writer refers to himself as one 'fra gli'altri uomini' – and the poem is addressed to a lady – 'a la sua donna'. The gender of the speaker in the passage that D'India sets is perhaps less explicitly expressed, though the beloved is, in fact, female and referred to both as 'reina' and 'dea'. The circumstances of Monteverdi's *lettera* and *partenza* – their use of clefs, placement in two different partbooks (in the Seventh Book of 1619) and pairing in the 1623 print – suggests that one should be sung by a soprano and the other by a tenor. In the case of D'India's *lettera* and several others in this period, it is technically possible for the pieces to be sung either by a soprano or a tenor one octave lower. The question is again about whether the singer acts as the writer of the letter, its reader, or, intriguingly, if the ambiguity is meant to suggest that the singer may ventriloquize and embody some combination of the two. The *lettera amorosa* by Filippo Vitali – 'Misero e pur convien occhi crudeli' – specifically indicates that the piece could be for either 'canto o tenore'.[146] Vitali's performance instruction implies that other love letters could also invite similar play both on perspective and gender. Neither Frescobaldi, in his 1630 setting of Preti's 'Vanne, o carta amorosa', nor Benedetto Ferrari (*c*. 1603–81), in his *lettera amorosa* 'Scrivete là dentro a que' fogli eterni' of 1637, explicitly indicates the intended voice type. The generic designation 'a voce sola' may have naturally lent itself to a variety of different vocal ranges, but the perspectival peculiarities of the *lettera amorosa* make the choice particularly transformative in performance.

The question of gender, though a subtle and complex one in any of the *lettere amorose* seen thus far, is perhaps most overtly evoked in 'Misero e pur convien', a *lettera amorosa* by the Florentine composer Filippo Vitali (1590–1654). The anonymous epistolary text in *versi sciolti* focuses almost entirely upon the guilt of the lady to whom it is addressed: 'questo vergato foglio | è di tua infedeltà misero esempio' ('this lined paper is of your infidelity a miserable example').[147] A woman by the name of Clorinda is accused in writing of being inconstant and unfaithful,

---

[146] Vitali's *lettera amorosa* is included in his *Concerto. Madrigali et altro generi di canti ... Libro primo* (1629); the piece is prefaced by the rubric 'Lettera amorosa a voce sola e canta senza Battuta. Canto o Tenore'.

[147] The piece is mentioned briefly in Racek, *Stilprobleme der italienischen Monodie*, p. 72.

her cruelty made all the more unjustified in the face of an innocent and pure heart upon which her letter-writing lover prides himself (Online Appendix 4.2a).[148]

Although the text echoes the *concettismo* of Achillini more than it hearkens back to the Latin verse of Ovid, the performative situation of a woman unwittingly binding herself in the act of reading strongly recalls the story of Cydippe and Acontius seen in Section 1. When Cydippe reads Acontius's letter aloud she becomes contractually bound to its contents whether they be a true reflection of reality or not. In Vitali's *lettera*, she is coerced into performing the accusatory words of another, and by her own voice, those words become both true and binding.

Whereas D'India skipped most of Marino's similarly chilling accusations of infidelity, Vitali's *lettera amorosa* focuses upon it and magnifies the transformative power of musical performance. The question of who is singing is once again the crux of the issue. A tenor may certainly perform this piece, as Vitali's own rubric concedes. If one assumes that the male voice is the writer, this might suggest a situation in which a frustrated lover expresses his incomprehensible feelings, feelings that he wishes his beloved could understand but he cannot bring himself to tell her. The performance of 'writing' would therefore represent a kind of emotional catharsis, for a letter written in moments of confusion and anguish is not necessarily a letter sent. A passage later in Vitali's text expresses the (unfulfilled?) wish that the beloved may see the trembling hand that writes: 'Ah, se vedessi, o Dio | quella man che tremante con quest'estremi inchiostri | scopre dell'amor mio gl'eccessi orrendi' ('Ah, if you [second person singular] could have seen, o God!, this hand that, trembling with these fatal ink strokes, reveals the horrible excesses of my love'). If the letter should, however, be performed by a soprano as the recipient of the letter, the whole situation would be cast in a different light. The lady, in receipt of the letter, narrates the details of her own guilt and, like Cydippe, has her own voice commandeered in the service of another man's feelings. The stakes for the women are, here as in Ovid, considerably higher. A soprano as the letter's recipient does, however, exert some emotional control over the words when the letter is performed as a monody. For even if the words are not her own, she is in control of the pacing and the execution of Vitali's musical and gestural affects.

The issue of gender is therefore more fluid than it seems when a written love letter becomes a musical performance. Even if the text suggests that the writer is male and the recipient female, the gender of the singer alone does not necessarily determine how the perspective of the poem is meant to be understood. What matters is the way the audience understands the voice of the performer. If this is a letter from a man to a woman, as the words suggest, which role does the singer,

---

[148] Upon the second mention of the lady's name the canto partbook gives the name 'Dorinda' instead of 'Clorinda'; the *partitura* partbook gives the name consistently as 'Clorinda'.

as a soprano or a tenor, embody? The performance may imply one reading even if the text implies another; a castrato may sing in the soprano range, or the letter could be interpreted as one from one woman to another. And the perspective need not remain stable; it may change mid-piece, for the voice itself is not exclusively tied to one perspective. This is even more so the case if the voice is tied to a nebulous 'her', which could be a woman as much as it could be an inanimate object: *la lettera* herself. There is no reason to suppose that the composer intended to solve the perspectival ambiguities afforded by the *lettera amorosa* – quite the contrary, in fact. The performance of Vitali's *lettera* by a tenor or a soprano affords multiple readings of the text that can coexist, and even simultaneously.

Vitali's *lettera amorosa* is in several respects a response to Monteverdi. Though the issue of gender is given over to the choice of the performer much more directly in Vitali (or D'India), the integrated perspectival ambiguity nevertheless draws clear inspiration from Monteverdi. As mentioned, Vitali's 1629 collection, *Concerto ... Madrigali et altri generi di canti*, is clearly modelled on Monteverdi's Seventh Book, while the *lettera amorosa* itself bears the same designation given to Monteverdi's love letter: 'in genere rappresentativo e si canta senza battuta'. What is more, the text of 'Misero e pur convien, occhi crudeli' is parsed into sections delineated by fermatas in much the same way that Monteverdi structured his *lettera* and *partenza* (Example 13). Though the poet of Vitali's poem is unknown, there are some clear allusions to Achillini's text set by Monteverdi. The 'letters' are once again notes staining the page that the beloved is invited to look at ('rimiri'), as if it were once again a mirror image of the lover's heart. The reappearance of the word 'stille' – also striking in Achillini's *lettera*, creates an uncomfortably visceral image of blood being filtered through the lover's heart onto the page (see Online Appendix 4.2b).

The image of a heart that oozes or drips with blood on account of lovesickness is powerful, and here, as in Achillini's poem, the word 'stille' from the verb 'stillare' – to distil or filter – is equally striking. The letter is the transfigured, love-changed heart of the writer: the product of an externalized soul sent forth as ink on paper to entreat a response. The line 'che sotto forma d'infelice inchiostro' bears a strong resemblance to the opening of Achillini's *lettera*, here once again underscoring the sensory transformation of the lover's heart into letters on the page. The drops of blood that pour out the lover's heart ('stille di sangue, | che con la penna ogn'hor versa il cor mio') are in fact the infinite marks ('punt'infiniti') which, under the guise of that unhappy ink, make his torments both visible and legible ('si scorgono tremanti, | si leggono dolenti').

We have seen that the *lettera amorosa* may 'represent' many of the interrelated facets of epistolary communication. Depending on how the pieces are performed, the music may represent the act of writing, typically a male writer to his lady, or

Lettera amorosa

Example 13 Filippo Vitali, 'Misero e pur convien, occhi crudeli', mm. 1–37

Example 13 (Cont.)

the act of reading, if the beloved reads the words written to her. This versatility of interpretation is certainly the case in the *lettere amorose* of Monteverdi, D'India, and Vitali. Love letters may also be poetic conceits, 'sent', perhaps, to their recipients but addressed self-reflexively, as seen in the madrigals of Marino, or the monodic 'Vanne, o carta amorosa' by Frescobaldi.[149]

The *lettera amorosa* of Frescobaldi is peculiar. Its text is a lengthy poem in *versi sciolti* and the music, a piece for solo voice in a declamatory style that opens the composer's *Secondo libro d'arie musicali* (1630), is much closer to the letters of Monteverdi, D'India, and Vitali discussed here. And yet the subject matter of the text is in some respects similar to the *concettismo* of the epistolary madrigals discussed in Section 2. The poem first appears in Girolamo Preti's *Idilli e rime* (1614) and, like Claudio Achillini's 'Se i languidi miei sguardi' set by Monteverdi, 'Vanne, o carta amorosa' is also labelled 'idillio'.[150] The *argomento* reveals that the text is a letter written by a timid lover who has decided to reveal the secret of his love to his lady but, not having the courage to speak of this to more than one person and because he has not received news from his beloved, resolves to live miserably.[151] Neither the *argomento* nor the contents of the poem, in which the lover describes in great detail the suffering of his love, make it clear whether this letter was actually meant to be sent or if it is a kind of virtuoso meditation on what he would say if he had the courage to do so. The text clearly indicates that this is in fact a love letter but, like some of the shorter epistolary poems seen in Section 2, the words are those of the lover speaking not to his beloved but to the letter itself. Even then, the words may or may not be the contents of an actual letter. The author wills the paper to go as his ambassador and as a kind of token of himself; the letter may carry the words he is not, for various reasons, able to speak to her himself. He cannot ask anything of her, but the letter can: 'chiedi, chiedi a colei'.[152] The text is a sort of self-reflexive letter about a letter, or, put another way, a representation of a representation (online Appendix 4.3).

Frescobaldi's musical setting of Preti's letter does not explicitly indicate the intended voice type although it is, like Monteverdi's letter, notated in C1 clef suggesting a higher voice. The performance of the poetry leaves the listeners to decide whether our timid lover's letter was actually sent and, of course, who is singing. The text seems to bypass the lady altogether, however, and the letter's contents, if that is in fact what listeners assume they are hearing, are a conversation between the letter writer and his pen-and-ink emissary. One could assume that the

---

[149] 'Vanne o carta amorosa' was also set by Giovanni Valentini in his *Muische a2* (1622); he also set 'Questa candida carta' in his *Quinto libro de madrigali* (1625). A *lettera amorosa* by Agostino Facchi, 'Vanne, diletto foglio', appeared in his *Madrigali a2–5* (1625), a copy of which is preserved at Mdina Cathedral, Malta; see Bisazza, 'The Madrigals of Agostino Facchi'; and Bruni, 'Seventeenth-Century Music Prints at Mdina Cathedral, Malta', pp. 467–79.

[150] Preti, *Idilli e rime*, pp. 51–62.

[151] A later print of Preti's collected works gives the poem the additional title of 'L'Amante timido'; *Poesie di Girolamo Preti* (Rome: Facciotti, 1625), pp. 263–79.

[152] It's worth recalling that the earliest print of Achillini's 'Se i languidi miei sguardi' appears in the 1612 *L'amorosa ambasciatrice* (Vicenza: Grossi, 1612), pp. 7–14.

singer is the letter's potential recipient if she is female, but if the letter was never sent the situation is more peculiar. The 'voice' of the letter cannot, in this case, be the letter itself since it is clearly written from the perspective of the writer, a writer who tells the letter that he does not in fact want his lady to love him because love is torture. He does not ask for her love in return, merely that she receives word of his sufferings and permits him to love her without reciprocation. Her role in this little intrigue is, potentially for practical reasons, as an amorous placeholder. And yet the voice of the singer is still nebulous. Even if the letter does not 'speak' directly, its voice is described in a passage not set by Frescobaldi. The letter may speak 'silently' and that is its advantage ('deh, potessi tu allhora | a lei ridire i miei sospir tacendo'), and so he may write ('deh, scriver potess'io | sì come le parole, anco i sospiri') in order to speak freely, like his letter, without any consequence.[153] Like Sappho's riddle, quoted at the outset of Section 1, a letter is powerful because it can communicate privately without being overheard. And yet as a musical piece, it is forcibly given a voice and is, by definition, a public performance.[154]

The opening of Frescobaldi's 'Vanne, o carta amorosa' suggests, as do many musical love letters of the period, a rhythmic and metrical freedom in its delivery (Example 14). As we have seen, the erotic paradox of the love letter suggests the impossible possibility of manipulating not only perspective but distance and time. Although in this instance Frescobaldi does not, as do Monteverdi and Vitali, indicate explicitly that the *lettera amorosa* should be sung 'senza battuta', he does refer precisely to this kind of freedom in the preface to his 1615 book of keyboard toccatas.

> Primieramente: che non de[v]e questo modo di sonare stare soggetto a battuta, come veggiamo usarsi ne i Madrigali moderni, i quali quantunque difficili si agevolano per mezzo della battuta portandola hor languida, hor veloce, e sostenendola etiandio in aria secondo i loro affetti, o senso delle parole.[155]
>
> Firstly, that this mode of playing should not remain subject to the beat, [but rather] should follow the manner of modern madrigals, in which any number of difficulties are made easier by carrying the beat now slowly, now quickly, and suspending it in the air according to their affects, or the sense of the words.[156]

---

[153] A queste voci, o carta, | se vedrai, che risplenda | solo un raggio di sdegno in quel bel volto: | allhor taci, ne intenda | altra voce da te, che questa, ei muore. | Deh, potessi tu allhora | a lei ridire i miei sospir tacendo: | deh scriver potess'io | sì, come le parole, anco i sospiri'; Preti, *Idilli e rime*, p. 55; *Poesie*, pp. 267–68.

[154] One may again recall the anxieties about vocalization expressed by the letters of Ovid's heroines in the *Heroides*.

[155] Frescobaldi, *Toccate e partite d'intavolatura di cimbalo*.

[156] Translation in Cypess, '*Esprimere la voce humana*', 181–223 (p. 191).

Example 14 Girolamo Frescobaldi, 'Vanne, o carta amorosa', mm. 1–9

The implication here is that the *genere ruppresentativo*, though clearly associated with music for voice and vocality in general was also conceived of instrumentally, conveys a paradox in representation. 'Representative' ambiguity is, as we have seen, the primary characteristic of the *lettera amorosa*.

One final example from this period illustrates yet another imaginative perspectival triangulation created when an epistle is sung as a musical piece. If

Vitali's 'Misero e pur convien, occhi crudeli' should be performed by the letter's recipient – the woman to whom the words are addressed – she, as the singer, would effectively be reading out the terms of her own guilt for an audience to hear and interpret as they will. Benedetto Ferrari's *lettera amorosa* – 'Scrivete là dentro a quei fogli eterni' – presents a rather different twist on this erotic triangulation between writer, reader, and listener. This anonymous text, included in Ferrari's second book of *Musiche varie* (1637), is not a transcript of a letter, and nor does it use the letter as a self-reflexive conceit.[157] The words of the sonnet, which are in the voice of some unnamed narrator, instruct someone else in the imperative to write by dictation (online Appendix 4.4).

The letter itself is in praise of yet a third person: a woman by the name of Lidia. Though the piece uses a C1 clef, implying a performance by a higher voice, this unusual situation makes the position of the singer fundamentally ambiguous in relation to the other people implied by the text. If she is presumably Lidia, then would this mean that instead of having her voice commandeered, as was the case in Vitali's *lettera*, here it is her hand and pen? Is she validating someone else's love for her not only with her voice but by the act of inscribing it on paper? Even if we assume that the singer takes on the persona of the poetic 'I' – the person dictating the words – this would create a scenario in which the narrator, who may or may not be in love with Lidia, is telling someone else to write down their words in praise of her. Who is the mysterious writer to whom the narrator speaks, and what do they have to do with Lidia? Or perhaps the text is in fact self-reflexive, as the writer 'speaks' to himself (or herself), urging themselves to write down what is difficult to say aloud. This kind of 'writing' is, however, much more abstract than in early *lettere amorose*; the act of writing is in this case an analogy for fate, a metaphor for the inscription of destiny.

Ferrari's *lettera* begins with an emphatic opening: the imperative command 'Scrivete là' ('write there') is set with a striking pair of upward leaps that bring the singer immediately to the top end of their range (Example 15). The way the music is left momentarily hanging on the top g″ breathlessly captures the listener's attention focusing it on both the ambiguity of the command itself – who is speaking? – and on the act of writing – who is doing the writing? The first few seconds of the piece therefore already encapsulate the perspectival and sensory paradoxes of the mode: the letter, though in this case written by someone else, is the worldly distillation of the lover's otherworldly soul. To write may be just as figurative as it is literal. That Ferrari saw music occupying this liminal space between material and

---

[157] Ferrari, known primarily as a composer of opera, dedicated his *Musiche varie a voce sola ... Libro secondo* to Basil Fielding, 2nd Earl of Denbigh, the English ambassador to the Republic of Venice. The piece 'Scrivete là dentro a que' fogli eterni' is prefaced by the rubric 'Poesia D'incerto'.

Example 15 Benedetto Ferrari, 'Scrivete là dentro a que' fogli eterni', mm. 1–11

immaterial is reflected in his dedicatory preface in which he writes 'music is an extract of human pleasures; the mortal on earth enjoys it, the blessed in heaven are satisfied with it'.[158]

---

[158] 'La Musica è un estratto, dell'humane dolcezze; ne gode il mortale in terra, se n'appaga il Beato nel Cielo'; Benedetto Ferrari, *Musiche varie a voce sola*.

Example 16 Ferrari, 'Scrivete là dentro a que' fogli eterni', mm. 26–44

Although the music of Ferrari's *lettera* is almost entirely virtuosic recitative the poem is, as Silke Leopold has remarked, a sonnet and thus unusual in its fixed structure when compared to many other texts set as musical love letters.[159] Although Ferrari's vocal writing shows few signs of regularity or repetition – the *passaggi* are free in their intricate ornamentation – the first half of the sestet presents a notable exception; here Ferrari switches to a brief passage in strict and regular triple time. The amorous melodiousness of the change seems to convey, by means of its opposite, the bellicoseness of the text: the time change occurs on the words 'S'armi, s'armi', referring to the proud 'armaments' with which fate leads the unfortunate lover to his death. The music may signify love and life even as the words convey war and death. Even more striking is the contrast between the most irregular image of the letter – the wind that indiscriminately blows the author's ashes away – and the ordered triple-time climax that leaves 'il vento' hanging once again at the highest part of the vocal tessitura (Example 16). As a representation of a written document, the performance of a love letter enacts the illusion that nature's most uncontrollable forces can somehow be controlled: if the act of writing rationalizes life into law, then the act of singing rationalizes love itself.

---

[159] Leopold, *Al modo d'Orfeo*, pp. 182–84.

5 The Epistolary Cantata

Nearly two centuries after the love letters of Tebaldeo and Tromboncino, the *lettera amorosa* continued to have a curious appeal even as it was adapted, both practically and aesthetically, to new historical and performative circumstances. Whether as prose, poetry, or painting, the epistolary remained a visceral and timeless mirror for the contradictory emotions of writers and recipients. That a letter could embody multiple spaces and times, senses, and perspectives, made it particularly apt to convey the ambiguity of consciousness. The letter, as a stylized adaptation of changing methods of communication, endured even in the new styles and genres of the late seventeenth and early eighteenth centuries. In his description of the *lettera amorosa*, the Florentine music theorist Giovan Battista Doni attempted in vain to assign a distinctive style to epistolary music; the love letter traverses multiple styles and genres. But Doni did manage to communicate one of the most intriguing characteristics of the *lettera amorosa*: its ability in performance to fall somewhere between reciting and artful singing, just as the text falls somewhere between reading and writing: 'è un canto mezzano tra 'l recitare e il modulare artifiziosamente'.[160]

By the middle of the seventeenth century, the *lettera amorosa* had moved into new musical arenas: opera and the epistolary cantata. As Beth Glixon has shown, the letter became a dramatic convention in the plots of seventeenth-century Venetian operas. Letters were tools of deception, interception, and a way of circumventing proper channels of communication with 'silent' words on stage. The librettos of Nicolò Minato (*c.* 1627–98), written for Venice between mid century and the late 1660s, employed the device most readily. *Scipione affricano* (1664) and *Artemisia* (1656), set to music by Francesco Cavalli (1602–76), each use letters to advance the plot and communicate information that, for various reasons, could not or ought not be spoken in public. Whereas the texts of these operatic letters typically had a practical dramatic function, the *lettere amorose* we have seen so far are anything but practical and do not, for the most part, make sense within dramatic contexts. The particular artifice and convoluted vocality of the *lettera amorosa* endured not in the realm of opera but rather in the epistolary cantata of the mid to late seventeenth century.

At some point during the mid seventeenth century, perhaps around the time Vermeer painted 'The Love Letter', Roman composer Giacomo Carissimi

---

[160] The passage is from Doni's *Trattato della musica scenica* (1633–5), is quoted in Privitera, 'Leggete queste note', p. 246 and in Fabbri, *Monteverdi*, trans. Carter, p. 168. See also Solerti, *Le origini del melodramma*, pp. 218–19. Doni draws an analogy concerning, of all things, an otter; the composite musical language of the *lettere amorose* does not double up on pleasure, so says Doni, any more than does the otter give the pleasures of eating meat and fish at the same time, even if it is itself 'mezza pesce e mezza carne'. His distain for stylistic plurality may however be related more to his preference for music that directly serves a dramatic function.

(1605–74) set the love letter 'Scrivete, occhi dolenti' as a cantata for solo voice. The piece survives in a single manuscript and, as with most of Carissimi's cantatas, the exact date of composition is not certain.[161] The text of 'Scrivete, occhi dolenti' bears some similarity to that of Rinuccini's *partenza* 'Se pur destina e vòle' set by Monteverdi and discussed in Section 3, in that the focus is not so much on a transcript of a letter's contents but on the meditation of a lover communicating his torments.[162] The sensory and perspectival peculiarities of 'Scrivete, occhi dolenti' are, on the other hand, equally reflective of Monteverdi's *lettera amorosa* 'Se i languidi miei sguardi' on a text by Achillini.

Just as the beloved of Monteverdi's *partenza* 'speaks' to his own eyes, the lover of Carissimi's cantata begins by addressing his own 'occhi dolenti' whom he wills to 'write' his emotions by using tears as ink to the paper of his face. The eyes are, as in several other *lettera amorosa* texts, complicit in the pain caused to the lover but they are also agents that bring about the act of 'reading'.

Scrivete, occhi dolenti,	Write, pained eyes,
con inchiostro di pianto	in ink of tears
sul foglio del mio volto, i vostri affanni.	on the paper of my face, your troubles.
Narrate i miei tormenti,	Narrate my torments,
registrate i miei danni,	register my injuries,
e dite a chi nol crede,	and tell them who does not believe it,
ch'amar tacendo ogni martire eccede.	that to love in silence exceeds every martyrdom.[163]

The silence ('ch'amar tacendo') through which they love is literal – because this love is implied to be forbidden – though paradoxical in a musical performance. In the opening passage, Carissimi sets the imperative command 'scrivete' to an evocative upward leap very much like the gesture that opens both Monteverdi's *lettera* and *partenza*. The declamatory beginning gives way to triple time at 'con

---

[161] Only five of Carissimi's cantatas were published during his lifetime of which 'Scrivete, occhi dolenti' is not one (it survives only in I-Bc, ms. X. 235). During his tenure at the Jesuit Collegium Germanicum in Rome (and even after his death in 1674) very little of Carissimi's music was published and the vast majority of it survives in manuscript, if at all. Although it is known that Carissimi wrote cantatas between 1640 to 1672, very few pieces can be dated and, as Gloria Rose has suggested, the composer may have been writing secular music throughout his creative life. See Rose, 'The Cantatas of Giacomo Carissimi', 205–15 (p. 205).

[162] The literary tradition of writing books of fictional letters continued in the seventeenth century; see Favaro, 'La retorica della schiettezza', pp. 20–35.

[163] For a transcription of the music and translation of the text see Holzer, 'Music and Poetry in Seventeenth-Century Rome', pp. 933–45. A transcription is also included in Roger Freitas, '*Un Atto d'ingegno*', pp. 613–23. A modern edition of the piece can be found in Melani, *Complete Cantatas*.

Example 17 Giacomo Carissimi, 'Scrivete, occhi dolenti', mm. 1–13

inchiostro di pianto' as the text shifts from the source of the writing – the pained eyes – to the means and contents of what the eyes are communicating (Example 17).

By the end of the text, the address shifts to the lady herself, whom the beloved wills to 'read the notes' directed at her, or the 'message' traced by the tears on his pained face. The transformation from tears to ink and face to paper is complete as the letter is signed by fate and sealed in blood: 'sottoscritto da mio fato | sigillato dal mio sangue'. Although Carissimi's text is similar to the *partenza* in its focus on the sense of sight and the beloved's face, there is one important distinction. Whereas the speaker of Rinuccini's 'Se pur destina e vòle' implores its listeners to hear ('odi'), speak ('ridite'), and see ('rimira'), the author of 'Scrivete, occhi dolenti' instead asks them to read ('leggi') and respond ('rispondi') in the informal, second person address.

Leggi, deh leggi o bella	Read, please read, o beautiful lady,
le note a te dirette,	the notes addressed to you,
e se qualche pietà nel seno ascondi,	and if some pity hides in your breast,
con un breve rescritto	with a brief rescript
o di vita o di morte, almen rispondi.	respond to me at least, whether of life or death.

Despite this change of perspective, marked by Carissimi with a subtle shift to a more declamatory style, the majority of the text is, like Monteverdi's *partenza*, not a literal transcript of a letter but rather a stylized meditation on speaking without words. The consequences of this are performative: the reciprocity, or lack thereof, between the writer and the reader is not straightforward. Though Carissimi's music may, like many of the other monodic love letters seen in previous sections, be performed by a high or low voice despite the poetry's address to a woman, the text strongly suggests that the writer, in the act of 'writing', tries and fails to communicate to their beloved. The person performing those words may or may not be the writer commanding their eyes to write the words. The text of Carissimi's 'Scrivete, occhi dolenti' nevertheless encapsulates the sensory paradox so central to the *lettera amorosa*: if the look can narrate more readily than words, then the face itself becomes its epistolary proxy, or the mirror stands in for the reflection. The focus is on seeing rather than hearing, as words are clearly not enough, and the act of reading, which was metaphorical, becomes literal again: 'Sì, sì, taccia la lingua | ma favellino i lumi ... Occhi scrivete, e tu mia vita leggi' ('Yes, yes, let my tongue be silent, but let my eyes tell ... Eyes, you write, and you, my life, read'). Carissimi marks this change yet again with declamatory recitative in contrast to the previous section, which is in a melodious triple time (Example 18). The 'letter' is really the 'writing' on the beloved's face that can communicate more readily than words because the writing itself represents torments transfigured. In being 'read' these torments are then converted back by the very instruments that transformed them in the first place: the eyes not of the writer, but of the reader.

'Scrivete, occhi dolenti' was again set as a cantata some years later by the composer and castrato Atto Melani (1626–1714). It is the only piece by Melani that has a textual concordance.[164] The cantata survives in several sources, as traced in detail by Roger Freitas, but one manuscript source is of particular interest not least because it gives a poetic attribution. 'Scrivete, occhi dolenti' appears in a manuscript of Italian cantatas housed at the Bibliothèque Nationale de France (F-Pn, Rés., Vmf, ms. 41, ff. 61^r–72^r). It contains music by a variety of composers including Antonio Cesti, Alessandro Stradella, and Luigi Rossi.[165] The first page of Melani's 'Scrivete, occhi dolenti' tells us that the words are by the poet and librettist Giovani Filippo Apollonio (*c*. 1620–88). Though Apollonio did indeed author the words for many cantatas by Antonio Cesti and Alessandro Stradella, 'Scrivete, occhi dolenti' is not his poem but rather, as Robert Holzer has identified, that of Francesco Melosio (1609–70).[166] The text is included in Iseppo Prodocimo's edition of Melosio's works, the *Poesie e prose* of 1678, and,

---

[164] Freitas, '*Un Atto d'ingegno*', p. 382, 151n.
[165] The manuscript is fully digitized on Gallica and is a partially an autograph by Luigi Rossi.
[166] Holzer, 'Music and Poetry in Seventeenth-Century Rome', pp. 400–406.

Example 18 Carissimi, 'Scrivete, occhi dolenti', mm. 78–93

like Marino's *lettera*, bears the title 'Lettera alla S[ua] D[onna]'.[167] It may be a coincidence that the Paris manuscript mentioned above containing Melani's setting of 'Scrivete, occhi dolenti' bears the ornate ex-libris of the musicologist Henry Prunières (1886–1942), the author of a 1924 monograph on Monteverdi's music. But Melani's *lettera amorosa* nevertheless shares some practical similarities with the love letters of Monteverdi's time, and the connection with the earlier repertory might explain Prunières's interest. The Monteverdian connections seem even less coincidental when one considers that another manuscript of cantatas by Alessandro Stradella (1643–82)[168] – including three *lettere amorose* for solo soprano – was owned by Gian Francesco Malipiero (1882–1973), the first editor of Monteverdi's complete works.[169]

---

[167] Melosio, *Poesie e prose . . . parte terza*, pp. 83–84.

[168] A baptismal document rediscovered in 2018 by Davide Mingozzi places Stradella's birth date in 1643 rather than the previously hypothesized 1639; see Mingozzi, 'Alessandro Stradella "bononiensis dominus"', *Il Saggiatore musicale* 25, no. 2 (2018): pp. 299–308.

[169] Three love letters: 'Sopra candido foglio' (10ᵛ–12ʳ), 'Su quel candido foglio (34ʳ–38ʳ), and 'Vanne foglio amoroso (77ʳ–82ʳ) appear in a manuscript at the Biblioteca della Fondazione

The style of Melani's 'Scrivete, occhi dolenti' is certainly closer to Carissimi than it is Monteverdi, but both pieces are still closely connected to sensory and perspectival epistolary of the *lettera amorosa* tradition, adapted as cantatas instead of as madrigals. If Carissimi's cantata, like others from the earlier seventeenth century, could be adapted in practice for high or low voice, Melani's setting actually survives in two distinct versions: one for soprano in C minor and another for bass in A minor.[170] Melani's two versions of 'Scrivete, occhi dolenti' codify the performative ambiguity of *lettere amorose* from earlier in the century: even if the text in this case strongly suggests a meditation on the act of writing, the singer can nevertheless stand in for the reader, the writer, the letter itself, or all three at different times. Like Carissimi, Melani sets parts of the text in an aria-like triple time though perhaps in a more circumscribed and straightforward way than his older contemporary. The middle section of the text – in which we hear what the eyes have 'written' in the first person – is in Melani's version crafted as aria made of *ottonari* whereas the beginning and end are in more irregular recitative to suit the *versi sciolti*. The aria ends at 'Leggi, deh leggi o bella' (see text above), at which point Melani marks the shift in perspective with a return to a declamatory style. What was in the earlier *lettera amorosa* an opportunity to suggest the ambiguity of perspective possible in the performance of a letter is here indicated by the increased polarization between aria and recitative. But the duality of perspective still seems to flow naturally from the dual nature of the epistolary mode, as words written and received, even if it does so in more clearly demarcated stylistic terms.

The end of Melani's cantata very clearly indicates the shift in voice by a contrast in musical style to show that the text is now specifically directed at a beautiful lady, whom the writer instructs in the imperative to 'read' ('leggi'). Still, Melani hints, in a subtle and perhaps less destabilizing way than some of his predecessors, that the opposing perspective – the love song of the aria section – is spoken and sounded simultaneously. This final passage (Example 19), while beginning as a recitative, also contains a subdued reminiscence of the triple time for the final supplication: 'o di vita o di morte almen rispondi' ('respond to me at least whether for life or for death'). The 'written' reply is given a voice by the ventriloquized hope of the letter

---

Giorgio Cini in Venice (I-Vgc, MAL.T.272) which belonged to Gian Francesco Malipiero (1882–1973). The manuscript's contents have been studied in detail by Giovani, 'Un manoscritto sconosciuto', 283–323 (pp. 298–99). A detailed description can also be found in the online database CLORI: Archivio della cantata italiana.

[170] See notes by Freitas that list the manuscript sources for each version; Melani, *Complete Cantatas*, pp. 60–72 and pp. 103–104.

Example 19 Atto Melani, 'Scrivete, occhi dolenti' (soprano version), mm. 182–206

writer. There is also a subtle but striking alteration to the text in Melani's version when compared to Carissimi: where the penultimate line in Carissimi reads 'con un *breve* rescritto ... almen rispondi' in which the writer asks the beloved for a *brief* written response, Melani's requests instead a *mute* yet still written reply – 'con un *muto* rescritto' – signalling the paradox of the letter as both silent and sounded. One may recall Sappho's riddle, quoted at the outset of Section 1, in which the letter is that 'creature' which is 'voiceless' but can still 'speak' to people far away.

The *lettera amorosa* endured in the cantata repertory of the late seventeenth and early eighteenth centuries, and its texts became codified into recitatives and arias: whole cantatas stood in for letters, their contents and, intriguingly, their (hoped for) responses. The aforementioned cantatas of Alessandro Stradella meditate on the letter as mirror for the soul sent forth to be graced by the beloved's eyes. The Venetian manuscript owned by Malipiero has three such letters, each focused on a different facet of the *lettera amorosa*: 'Sopra candido foglio' and 'Su quel candido foglio' are written from the female perspective, while 'Vanne, foglio amoroso' is written from the male one.[171] The epistolary cantatas of the late seventeenth and early eighteenth centuries reflect a manuscript culture (in contrast to the earlier printed *lettera amorosa* repertory) and, by the turn of the new century, tended to be organized in sets of letters and their responses.[172] A series of three cantata texts – 'Piangete, occhi dolenti', 'Tinte a note di sangue', and 'Scritte con falso inganno' – was set to music by the Neapolitan composer Francesco Mancini (1672–1737) and, a few decades later, by Domenico Scarlatti (1685–1757). The manuscript preserving Mancini's settings for solo soprano, now in the Biblioteca del Conservatorio di musica S. Pietro a Majella, dates the piece precisely to February 1716 and gives the letter the title *Pietà richiesta* ('Compassion requested').[173] In comparison with Scarlatti's later setting, Mancini's *lettera* is more overtly chromatic. The cantata begins with the author instructing her own eyes to cry so as to leave traces on the paper; the first 'piangete' is set by Mancini with a poignant if painful upward leap of a tritone (Example 20).[174]

---

[171] See Giovani, 'Un manoscritto sconosciuto', pp. 307–309 and pp. 314–16. 'Vanne foglio amoroso' is included in a modern edition, ed. Giovani, *Sei cantate a voce sola dal manoscritto appartenuto a Gian Francesco Malipiero*. The text for Stradella's 'Sopra candido foglio' refers to the character of Oronta, which as Francesco Degrada has suggested, might be making homage to *l'Orontea* (1656) of Antonio Cesti with a libretto by Giacinto Andrea Cicognini. See Degrada, 'Tre "lettere amorose" di Domenico Scarlatti', 271–316 (p. 288).

[172] There are several other epistolary cantatas from this period; see for instance 'Queste vermiglie note' by Giovanni Bononcini (1670–1747); 'Oh de miei lunghi e tormentosi afanni' by Antonio Caldara (*c*.1671–1736) and another setting of the same by Benedetto Marcello (1686–1739); and 'Vanne foglio fortunato' by Sebastiano Enno (*c*.1655). For full details see CLORI.

[173] See details of the source (I-Nc, Cantate 41 [14], ff. 104^r–107^v) on CLORI. There is another cantata by Mancini with the same incipit also preserved in Naples: I-Nc, Cantate 181 (35), ff. 117^r–121^r.

[174] Degrada conducts a comparative analysis between Mancini and Scarlatti's settings of this text; see Degrada, 'Tre "lettere amorose" di Domenico Scarlatti', p. 296.

Example 20 Francesco Mancini, 'Piangete, occhi dolenti', mm. 1–13

Piangete, occhi dolenti;	Weep, sad eyes;
al[175] vostro pianto imprima	let your tears stain
su d'un languido foglio i miei lamenti.	my laments onto this languid letter.
Piangete, occhi dolente;	Weep, sad eyes,
con note di dolore	with notes of pain
palesate gli affanni,	reveal my grief,
con cifre di pietade	with piteous figures
registrate i tormenti.	register my torments,
Piangete, occhi dolenti.	weep, sad eyes.

The latest musical love letters in this period are those by Domenico Scarlatti and, if less chromatic than earlier epistolary music, they are nevertheless

---

[175] In Scarlatti's setting: 'il'.

exquisitely virtuosic in every sense. Scarlatti's epistolary cantatas are, as Francesco Degrada has suggested, important witnesses to the composer's later stylistic and representational approach and reveal important connections between his vocal music and the much more widely known keyboard works.[176] Scarlatti's set of cantatas, written sometime after 1730 and preserved in a manuscript now in Vienna, represents the crystallization of a tradition of epistolary music dating back to the poetic improvisations of the late fifteenth century. Even as the latest of the pieces that can be called *lettera amorosa*, Scarlatti's music nevertheless encapsulates some of the temporal, perspectival and sensory contradictions we have seen in earlier *lettere amorose*. Still, by the eighteenth century, 'the *lettera amorosa* presupposes an absence and substitutes for a presence: it is a fragile bridge made of paper, thrown between two solitudes'.[177] In his description of Scarlatti's cantatas, Degrada further characterizes a performative situation very much akin to the earlier *lettere amorose* of Monteverdi, Vitali, and Carissimi, among others: the music suddenly vivifies the absent letter writer into a speaking, palpitating entity, one who had been 'excluded from a direct communicative connection, and in the meantime evokes to the one who reads it the image of themselves, through the eyes of the one about whom the letter is written'.[178] As we have seen however, musical *lettere amorose* are, even in the eighteenth century, paradoxes of representation: they deliberately play with the perspectives embedded in the texts and, particularly in the earlier repertory, the representational possibilities for the singer do not stop at the dichotomy between writer and reader.

Although all three of Scarlatti's epistolary cantatas are for soprano, the texts convey two distinct perspectives: a woman who writes to her beloved, and a man who writes back. 'Piangete, occhi dolenti' is the lady writing about writing (Figure 9); 'Tinte a note di sangue' is the response is steeped, somewhat typically as we have seen, in accusations of infidelity; the final cantata 'Scritte con falso inganno' is the woman's last word, in which she addresses the accusations laid at her door. The cantatas make sense as a set – the letters even quote contested passages from previous ones, literally putting words in each other's mouths – but there is no reason why they cannot be performed in

---

[176] Degrada, 'Tre "lettere amorose" di Domenico Scarlatti', pp. 315–16. Degrada suggests the epistolary cantatas from the Viennese manuscript date from after 1730 or even 1735 (p. 310). He points also to another possible *lettera amorosa* by Domenico's father Alessandro – 'Quel Fileno infelice' – with which the younger composer might have been familiar, pp. 289–90.
[177] Degrada, 'Tre "lettere amorose" di Domenico Scarlatti', p. 283.
[178] Degrada, 'Tre "lettere amorose" di Domenico Scarlatti', p. 283. 'In altre parole, la lettera amorosa presuppone un'assenza e surroga una presenza: è un fragile ponte di carta gettato tra due solitudini, rende improvvisamente vivo, parlante, palpitante colui che è stato escluso da un rapporto diretto di comunicazione e nel contempo evoca a chi legge l'immagine di sé stesso vista con gli occhi di chi la lettera scrisse'.

Figure 9 Domenico Scarlatti, 'Piangete, occhi dolenti' (after 1730), Österreichische Nationalbibliothek, Mus. Hs.17664, f. 93^v

succession by the same singer. It would be logical to have one singer representing each of the characters in cantatas, but the texts themselves ventriloquize the voices of the other enough that such strict dramatic delivery or demarcation is not necessary in this context. In contrast to earlier *lettere amorose*, the clear stylistic alternation between recitatives and arias naturally creates a kind of exchange that in a way functions in the place of actual letters that the singers may be 'writing'. The *lettera amorosa* is, as we have seen, an opportunity to perform multiple perspectives at once and to transform, as the inky tears of the opening passage of 'Piangete, occhi dolenti' do, the unseen physical tokens of grief into the legible symbols for an absent lover. As in all *lettere amorose*, the music strives to overcome both time and space: the absent becomes present, voices are commingled, and the past is manipulated in the present.

Epilogue

The *lettera amorosa*, while both peculiar and usual in the history of music, endured in various guises and practices through many centuries. Its persistence can be explained in part because it makes manifest the irrationality and occasional impossibility of human desire and its musical representation; we often desire things that simply cannot be in ways that can be expressed only obliquely and, sometimes, in someone else's voice. As we have seen, a letter transformed into a performance can defy the laws of physics as readily as it can circumvent the right to reply. Even as it was reinvented in the variety of styles and cultural contexts seen in the preceding sections, epistolary music preserves the dynamic vocality inherited from the traditions of ancient Greece. The *lettera amorosa* exploits the expressive potential of the paradoxes of eros, just as it re-enacts the central contractual role of orality in social relations. Its performativity suggests that amorous communications, as written and especially as sung, can represent or even deliberately change the way in which words and voices exist in time. The desire to control – to perform and be performed – in the voice of another may indeed stem from the irrationality of erotic desire, but it can also come from an earnest desire for intimacy and closeness.

The music of letters represents a very particular kind of human intimacy, one that is not bound by the strictures of time and place, but still creates a mysterious, audible immediacy. Epistolary sounds have taken many forms in different historical contexts, but they all seem to capture a poignancy that combines intensity with nostalgia. They ground us in the present by bringing the past into closer proximity with the future. They provide the connective tissue between people in the revivification of those who are absent. William Hazlett (1778–1830) describes the profound interconnectedness of feeling associated with the sound of letters in the 'Letter-Bell', his final essay published posthumously in March 1831:

> As I write this, the Letter-Bell passes; it has a lively, pleasant sound with it, and not only fills the street with its importunate clamour, but rings clear through the length of many half-forgotten years. It strikes upon the ear, it vibrates to the brain, it wakes me from the dream of time, it flings me back upon my first entrance into life, the period of my first coming up to town, when all around was strange, uncertain, adverse – a hubbub of confused noises, a chaos of shifting objects – and when this sound alone, startling me with the recollection of a letter I had sent to the friends I had lately left, brought me as it were to myself, made me feel that I had links still connecting me with the universe, and gave me hope and patience to persevere.[179]

---

[179] Hazlitt, 'The Letter-Bell (1831)', p. 347.

Fictional letters have always been admired for their 'useless' beauty. But perhaps their 'usefulness' comes less from any sense of practicality but rather as studies in the complexities of human communication. A musical epistle allows sounds to travel over great distances, stabilizing the voice of the writer just enough that it may commingle with the voice of whomever reads it. It is a musical experiment through which the passage of time can be manipulated.[180] It achieves, in this sense, some semblance of immortality. This necessary illusion is, as the *lettera amorosa* communicates, the usefulness of the useless.[181]

---

[180] Eliot, 'Burnt Norton', p. 16.   [181] Ordine, *The Usefulness of the Useless*.

Bibliography

Achillini, Claudio. *Poesie*. Edited by Angelo Colombo. Parma: Archivio Barocco, 1991.
  L'amorosa ambasciatrice idilio del m. ill. & eccellentiss. signore C.A. Vicenza: Francesco Grossi, 1612.
Alighieri, Dante. *The New Life*. Edited by Evelyn Paul. Translated by Dante Gabriel Rossetti. Coventry: George G. Harrap, 1915.
Alpers, Svetlana. *The Art of Describing: Dutch Art of the Seventeenth Century*. Chicago: University of Chicago Press, 1984.
Aristotle, Longinus, Demetrius. *Poetics. Longinus: On the Sublime. Demetrius: On Style*. Translated by Stephen Halliwell, W. Hamilton Fyfe, Doreen C. Innes, and W. Rhys Roberts. Rev. Donald A. Russell, Loeb Classical Library 199. Cambridge, MA: Harvard University Press, 1995.
Bacchelli, Riccardo. 'Sulla *lettera amorosa* di Claudio Achillini e di Claudio Monteverdi'. *Forum italicum* 6, no. 1 (1972): 111–12.
  Versi e rime. Vicenza: Mondadori, 1972.
Banchieri, Adriano. *Vivezze di Flora e primavera* (1622). Edited by Lino Bianchi. Rome: De Santis, 1971.
Barthes, Roland. *A Lover's Discourse*. Translated by Richard Howard. New York: Hill and Wang, 2010.
Bisazza, Mario. 'The Madrigals of Agostino Facchi'. MPhil diss., University of Malta, 1998.
Bridgman, Nanie. 'Un manuscrit italien du début du XVIe siècle'. *Annales musicologiques* I (1953): 177–267.
Bruni, Antonio. *Epistole eroiche*. Rome: Facciotti, 1627.
Bruni, Franco. 'Seventeenth-Century Music Prints at Mdina Cathedral, Malta'. *Early Music* 27, no. 3 (1999): 467–79.
Calcagno, Mauro. *From Madrigal to Opera: Monteverdi's Staging of the Self*. Berkeley: University of California Press, 2012.
  'Monteverdi's *parole sceniche*'. *Journal of Seventeenth-Century Music* 9, no. 1 (2003).
Campbell-Smith, Duncan. *Masters of the Post: The Authorized History of the Royal Mail*. London: Allen Lane, 2011.
Cantaloube-Ferrieu, Lucienne. 'Du chant au chant'. *Europe* 705–706 (1988): 66–73.
Carson, Anne. *Eros the Bittersweet*. Campaign: Dalkey Archive Press, 2015.

Carter, Tim. *Monteverdi's Voices: A Poetics of the Madrigal*. New York: Oxford University Press, 2024.

Carter, Tim. 'Beyond Drama: Monteverdi, Marino, and the Sixth Book of Madrigals (1614)'. *Journal of the American Musicological Society* 69, no. 1 (2016): 1–46.

'Intriguing Laments: Sigismondo d'India, Claudio Monteverdi, and Dido *alla parmigiana* (1628)'. *Journal of the American Musicological Society* 49, no. 1 (1996): 32–69.

'Monteverdi, Early Opera and a Question of Genre: The Case of *Andromeda* (1620)'. *Journal of the Royal Musical Association* 137, no. 1 (2012): 1–34.

Monteverdi's Musical Theatre. New Haven: Yale University Press, 2002.

Monteverdi's Voices: A Poetics of the Madrigal. New York: Oxford University Press, 2024.

Ceresini, Giovanni. *Madrigali concertati a due tre e quattro voci*. Venice: Alessandro Vincenti, 1627.

Char, René. *La parole en archipel*. Paris: Gallimard, 1962.

Coppini, Aquilino *Il secondo libro della musica di Claudio Monteverdi . . . fatta spirituale*. Milan: Agostino Tradate, 1608.

Cox, Virginia. *Lyric Poetry by Women of the Italian Renaissance*. Baltimore: Johns Hopkins University Press, 2013.

Cypess, Rebecca. '*Esprimere la voce humana*: Connections between Vocal and Instrumental Music by Italian Composers of the Early Seventeenth Century'. *The Journal of Musicology* 27, no. 2 (2010): 181–223.

D'Accone, Frank A. 'Instrumental Resonances in a Sienese Vocal Print of 1515'. In *Le Concert des voix et des instruments à la Renaissance: Actes du XXXIVe Colloque International d'Études Supérieures de la Renaissance, 1–11 juillet 1991*, 333–59. Edited by Jean-Michel Vaccaro. Paris: CNRS, 1995.

D'India, Sigismondo. *Le Musiche a una e due voci, Libri I–V (1609–1623)*. Edited by John Joyce. Florence: Olschki, 1981.

Degrada, Francesco. 'Tre "lettere amorose" di Domenico Scarlatti'. *Il Saggiatore musicale* 4, no. 2 (1997): 271–316.

Donne, John. *The Complete Poems*. Edited by A. J. Smith. London: Penguin Books, 1996.

Doni, Giovanni Battista. *Annotazioni sopra il compendio de' generi, e de' modi della musica*. Rome: Andrea Fei, 1640.

Doni, Trattato della musica scenica (1633–5). In *Lyra Barberina*. 2 vols. Florence: Stamperia Imperiale, 1763; repr. Bologna: Forni, 1974.

Einstein, Alfred. 'La prima "lettera amorosa" in musica'. *La Rassegna musicale* 10, no. 1 (1937): 45–52.

Eisner, Martin. *Dante's New Life of the Book*. Oxford: Oxford University Press, 2021.

Eliot, Thomas Stearns. 'Burnt Norton'. In *Four Quartets (1943)*, pp. 13–20. New York: Mariner Books, 1971.

Fabbri, Paolo. *Monteverdi*. Translated by Tim Carter. New York: Cambridge University Press, 1994.

Farrell, Joseph. 'Reading and Writing the *Heroides*'. *Harvard Studies in Classical Philology* 98 (1998): 307–38.

Favaro, Maiko. 'La retorica della schiettezza: Sulle *Lettere amorose* (1642) di Girolamo Brusoni'. *The Italianist* 37, no. 1 (2017): 20–35.

Ferrari, Benedetto. *Musiche varie a voce sola*. Venice: Magni, 1637.

Freitas, Roger. '*Un Atto d'ingegno*: A Castrato in the Seventeenth Century'. PhD diss., Yale University, 1998.

Frescobaldi, Girolamo. *Toccate e partite d'intavolatura di cimbalo*. Rome: Borboni, 1615.

Gallico, Claudio. 'La *lettera amorosa* di Monteverdi e lo stile rappresentativo'. *Nuova rivista musicale italiana* 1 (1967): 287–302.

Garavaglia, Andrea. *Sigismondo D'India 'drammaturgo'*. Turin: De Sono, 2005.

Garfield, Simon. *To the Letter*. New York: Gotham Books, 2013.

Georis, Christophe. *Claudio Monteverdi 'letterato' ou les metamorphoses du texte*. Paris: Honoré Champion, 2013.

Giles, Roseen. 'Giambattista Marino's *L'Adone*: A Drama of Madrigals'. *The Italianist* 40, no. 3 (2020): 419–40.

Giovani, Giulia. 'Un manoscritto sconosciuto di cantate e arie di Alessandro Stradella conservato a Venezia'. *Studi musicali* 4 (2013): 283–323.

Giovani, Giulia, ed. *Sei cantate a voce sola dal manoscritto appartenuto a Gian Francesco Malipiero*. Kassel: Bärenreiter, 2015.

Guardiani, Francesco. *La meravigliosa retorica dell'Adone di G.B. Marino*. Florence: Olschki, 1989.

Hazlitt, William. 'The Letter-Bell (1831)'. In *Selected Essays of William Hazlitt*, 347–53. Edited by Geoffrey Keynes. London: The Nonsuch Press, 1934.

Heller, Wendy. *Animating Ovid: Opera and the Metamorphosis of Antiquity in Early Modern Italy*, forthcoming.

'Hypsipyle, Medea, and the Ovidian Imagination: Taming the Hero in Cavalli's *Giasone*'. In *Readying Cavalli's Operas for the Stage: Manuscript, Edition, Production*, 167–86. Edited by Ellen Rosand. Farnham: Ashgate, 2013.

'Ovid's Ironic Gaze: Voyeurism, Rape, and Male Desire in Cavalli's *La Calisto*'. In *Eroticism in Early Modern Europe*, 203–25. Edited by Bonnie Blackburn and Laurie Stras. Farnham: Ashgate, 2015.

Holzer, Robert. 'Music and Poetry in Seventeenth-Century Rome: Settings of the Canzonetta and Cantata Texts of Francesco Balducci, Domenico

Benigni, Francesco Melosio, and Antonio Abati'. PhD diss., University of Pennsylvania, 1990.

Jensen, Katharine Ann. *Writing Love: Letters, Women, and thse Novel in France, 1605–1776*. Carbondale: Southern Illinois University Press, 1995.

Jeppesen, Knud. *La Frottola*. Aarhus: Universitetsforlaget, 1968.

Johnson, William A. 'Toward a Sociology of Reading in Classical Antiquity'. *The American Journal of Philology* 121, no. 4 (2000): 593–627.

Kivy, Peter. *The Performance of Reading*. Chichester: Wiley-Blackwell, 2009.

Kong, Katherine. *Lettering the Self in Medieval and Early Modern France*. Cambridge: D.S. Brewer, 2010.

Leopold, Silke. *Al modo d'Orfeo: Dichtung und Musik im italienischen Sologesang des frühen 17. Jahrhunderts*. Laaber: Laaber-Verlag, 1995.

'Remigio Romano's Collection of Lyrics for Music'. *Proceedings of the Royal Musical Association* 110 (1983–84): 45–61.

Lesure, François. *Manuscrit italien de frottola (1502)*. Geneva: Minkoff, 1979.

Luisi, Francesco, ed. *Il secondo libro di frottola di Andrea Antico*. Rome: Pro Musica Studium, 1976.

MacNeil, Anne. '"A Voice Crying in the Wilderness": Issues of Authorship, Performance, and Transcription in the Italian Frottola'. *The Italianist* 40, no. 3 (2020): 463–76.

Marini, Biagio. *Madrigali et Symfonie (1618)*. Edited by Aurelio Bianco and Sara Dieci. Turnhout: Brepols, 2014.

Marino, Giambattista. *Lettere*. Edited by Marziano Guglielminetti. Turin: Einaudi, 1966.

La lira 1614. Edited by Luana Salvarani. Lavis: La Finestra, 2012.

La strage degli innocenti. Edited by Giovanni Pozzi. Turin: Einaudi, 1960.

The Massacre of the Innocents. Translated by Erik Butler. Cambridge, MA: Wakefield Press, 2015.

Melani, Atto. *Complete Cantatas*. Edited by Roger Freitas. Middleton, WI: A-R Editions, 2006.

Melosio, Francesco. *Poesie e prose . . . parte terza*. Venice: Iseppo Prodocimo, 1678.

Metzer, David. *Quotation and Cultural Meaning in Twentieth-Century Music*. Cambridge: Cambridge University Press, 2003.

Miller, Roark. 'New Information on the Chronology of Venetian Monody: The "Raccolte" of Remigio Romano'. *Music and Letters* 77, no. 1 (1996): 22–33.

Mingozzi, Davide. 'Alessandro Stradella "bononiensis dominus"'. *Il Saggiatore musicale* 25, no. 2 (2018): 299–308.

Murata, Margaret. 'Image and Eloquence: Secular Song'. In *The Cambridge History of Seventeenth-Century Music*, 378–425. Edited by Tim Carter and John Butt. Cambridge: Cambridge University Press, 2005.

Ordine, Nuccio. *The Usefulness of the Useless*. Translated by Alastair McEwan. Philadelphia: Paul Dry Books, 2017.

Ovid. *Art of Love*. Translated by J. H. Mozley. Rev. G. P. Goold, Loeb Classical Library 232. Cambridge, MA: Harvard University Press, 1929.

Epistulae Ex Ponto, Book 1. Translated by Jan Felix Gaertner. Oxford: Oxford University Press, 2005.

Heroides. Translated by Grant Showerman, Loeb Classical Library 41. Cambridge, MA: Harvard University Press, 1977.

Tristia. Ex Ponto. Translated by A. L. Wheeler. Revised by G. P. Goold, Loeb Classical Library 151. Cambridge, MA: Harvard University Press, 1924.

Plant, Ian M., ed. *Women Writers of Ancient Greece and Rome*. Norman: University of Oklahoma Press, 2004.

Preti, Girolamo. *Idilli e rime*. Venice: Bortoloti, 1614.

Privitera, Massimo. '*Leggete queste note*: la *lettera amorosa* di Achillini e Monteverdi'. In *Poesie* (1632), 225–46. Edited by Angelo Colombo. Rome: Edizioni di storia e letteratura, 2010.

Prizer, William F. *Courtly Pastimes*: T*he Frottole of Marchetto Cara*. Ann Arbor: UMI Research Press, 1980.

'Isabella d'Este and Lucrezia Borgia as Patrons of Music: The Frottola at Mantua and Ferrara'. *Journal of the American Musicological Society* 38, no. 1 (1985): 1–33.

'Paris, Bibliothéque Nationale MS Rés. Vm^7 676 and Music at Mantua'. In *Atti del XIV Congresso della Società Internazionale di Musicologia*, 235–39. Edited by Angelo Pompilio. Turin: EDT, 1990.

Racek, Jan. *Stilprobleme der italienischen Monodie*. Prague: Státní pedagogické nakladatelství, 1965.

Rawles, Richard. 'Simonides on Tombs, and the "Tomb of Simonides"'. In *Tombs of the Ancient Poets*: *Between Literary Reception and Material Culture*, 51–68. Edited by Nora Goldschmidt and Barbara Graziosi. Oxford: Oxford University Press, 2018.

Rimell, Victoria. *Ovid's Lovers*. Cambridge: Cambridge University Press, 2006.

Romano, Remigio. *Prima raccolta di bellissime canzonette musicali*. Vicenza: Angelo Salvadori, 1622.

Seconda raccolta di canzonette musicali. Vicenza: Angelo Salvadori, 1620.

Terza raccolta di bellissime canzoni. Vicenza: Salvadori, 1622.

Rosand, Ellen. *Monteverdi's Last Operas: A Venetian Trilogy*. Berkeley: University of California Press, 2007.

Rose, Gloria. 'The Cantatas of Giacomo Carissimi'. *The Musical Quarterly* 48, no. 2 (1962): 205–15.

Rosenmeyer, Patricia A. *Ancient Epistolary Fictions: The Letter in Ancient Greek Literature*. Cambridge: Cambridge University Press, 2001.

Russo, Emilio. 'Le lettere del Marino e la cultura di primo Seicento'. In *Epistolari dal Due al Seicento: Modelli, questioni ecdotiche, edizioni, cantieri aperti*, 661–84. Edited by Claudia Berra, Paolo Borsa, Michele Comelli, and Stefano Martinelli Tempesta. Milan: Università degli studi di Milano, 2018.

Sacchi, Guido. 'Schede secentesche'. *Studi secenteschi* 43 (2002): 313–55.

Schrade, Leo. *Monteverdi: Creator of Modern Music*. New York: W.W. Norton, 1950.

Seneca the Younger. *Epistles, Volume I*. Translated by Richard M. Gummere, Loeb Classical Library 75. Cambridge, MA: Harvard University Press, 1917.

Slim, H. Colin. 'Valid and Invalid Options for Performing Frottole'. In *Painting and Music in the Sixteenth Century*, 317–31. Aldershot: Ashgate, 2002.

Solerti, Angelo. *Le origini del melodramma*. Turin: Fratelli Bocca, 1903.

Spentzou, Efrossini. *Readers and Writers in Ovid's Heroides: Transgressions of Genre and Gender*. Oxford: Oxford University Press, 2003.

Stanley, Liz. 'The Death of the Letter? Epistolary Intent, Letterness and the Many Ends of Letter-Writing'. *Cultural Sociology* 9, no. 2 (2015): 240–54.

Strunk, Oliver. *Source Readings in Music History, Vol. 4: The Baroque Era*. Edited by Margaret Murata. New York: W. W. Norton, 1998.

Sutton, Peter C., Lisa Vergara, and Ann Jensen Adams. *Love Letters: Dutch Genre Paintings in the Age of Vermeer*. London: Frances Lincoln, 2003.

Svenbro, Jesper. *Phrasikleia: An Anthropology of Reading in Ancient Greece*. Translated by Janet Lloyd. New York: Cornell University Press, 1993.

Tebaldeo, Antonio. *Rime*. Edited by Tania Basile and Jean-Jacques Marchand. Modena: Edizioni Panini, 1989.

Tomlinson, Gary. 'Music and the Claims of Text'. *Critical Inquiry* 8, no. 3 (1982): 565–89.

van Veen, Otto. *Amorum emblemata*. Antwerp: Verdussen, 1608.

Whenham, John. *Duet and Dialogue in the Age of Monteverdi*. Ann Arbor: UMI Research Press, 1982.

Wilson, Blake. *Singing the Lyre in Renaissance Italy: Memory, Performance, and Oral Poetry*. Cambridge: Cambridge University Press, 2020.

Acknowledgements

I am very grateful to Tim Carter, Claire Catenaccio, Robert Holzer, and Eugenio Refini for their insights, comments, and suggestions during the preparation of this manuscript.

Cambridge Elements

Music, 1600–1750

Rebecca Herissone
University of Manchester

Rebecca Herissone is Professor of Musicology at the University of Manchester and a Fellow of the British Academy. She is also a Vice-President of the Royal Musical Association, Chair of the Musica Britannica Editorial Committee and a member of several Editorial Boards. Her research focuses on the music of early modern England, particularly issues of creativity, material culture and reception. She has published three monographs, most recently the award-winning *Musical Creativity in Restoration England*, and articles in a wide range of international journals. She is currently working towards an interdisciplinary study of the material traces of Purcell's reception.

Daniel R. Melamed
Indiana University (Emeritus)

Daniel R. Melamed is Professor Emeritus of Musicology at the Indiana University Jacobs School of Music and Director of the Bloomington Bach Cantata Project. He has served as editor of the *Journal of Musicology* and president of the American Bach Society. With Michael Marissen he is the creator of BachCantataTexts.org, a free source of historically informed translations for the music of J. S. Bach. His books include *J. S. Bach and the German Motet*, *Hearing Bach's Passions*, and *Listening to Bach: The Mass in B Minor and the Christmas Oratorio*.

About the Series

This series offers new perspectives on how music was created, performed, heard and understood within the rich and vibrant cultures of the seventeenth and early eighteenth centuries. Cutting across national boundaries and genre distinctions, it explores both professional and recreational music-making in a wide range of social and geographical contexts.

Cambridge Elements

Music, 1600–1750

Elements in the Series

Lettera amorosa: *Musical Love Letters in Early Modern Italy*
Roseen Giles

A full series listing is available at: www.cambridge.org/EMSE

For EU product safety concerns, contact us at Calle de José Abascal, 56–1°,
28003 Madrid, Spain or eugpsr@cambridge.org.

www.ingramcontent.com/pod-product-compliance
Ingram Content Group UK Ltd.
Pitfield, Milton Keynes, MK11 3LW, UK
UKHW021326180426
11947UKWH00017B/1459